Spelling
Lessons and Activities

- **Word Lists**
- **Instruction**
- **Practice**
- **Extension and Enrichment**

HOLT, RINEHART AND WINSTON

A Harcourt Education Company

Orlando • **Austin** • New York • San Diego • Toronto • London

EDITORIAL

Manager of Editorial Operations

Bill Wahlgren

Executive Editors

Emily G. Shenk, Patricia A. McCambridge

Project Editors

James E. Eckel, Karen H. Kolar

Writing and Editing:

Karen S. Ellis, Michael Nassoiy

Editorial Assistant:

Kim Soriano

Copyediting:

Michael Neibergall, *Copyediting Manager;* Mary Malone, *Senior Copyeditor;* Joel Bourgeois, Elizabeth Dickson, Gabrielle Field, Julie A. Hill, Jane Kominek, Millicent Ondras, Theresa Reding, Dennis Scharnberg, Kathleen Scheiner, Laurie Schlesinger, *Copyeditors*

Project Administration:

Marie Price, *Managing Editor;* Lori De La Garza, *Editorial Operations Coordinator;* Thomas Browne, Heather Cheyne, Mark Holland, Marcus Johnson, Jill O'Neal, Joyce Rector, Janet Jenkins, Kelly Tankersley, *Project Administration;* Gail Coupland, Ruth Hooker, Margaret Sanchez, *Word Processing*

Editorial Permissions:

Janet Harrington, *Permissions Editor*

ART, DESIGN AND PHOTO

Graphic Services

Kristen Darby, *Manager*

Image Acquisitions

Joe London, *Director;* Tim Taylor, *Photo Research Supervisor;* Rick Benavides, *Assistant Photo Researcher;* Elaine Tate, *Supervisor;* Erin Cone, *Art Buyer*

Cover Design

Curtis Riker, *Director*

Sunday Patterson, *Designer*

PRODUCTION/ MANUFACTURING

Belinda Barbosa Lopez, *Senior Production Coordinator*

Carol Trammel, *Production Supervisor*

Beth Prevelige, *Senior Production Manager*

Table of Contents

How to Study a Word

1 SAY the word.
Remember when you have heard the word used.
Think about what it means.

2 LOOK at the word.
Find any prefixes, suffixes, or other word parts you know.
Think about other words that are related in meaning and
spelling. Try to picture the word in your mind.

3 SPELL the word to yourself.
Think about the way each sound is spelled. Notice any
unusual spelling.

4 WRITE the word while you are looking at it.
Check the way you have formed your letters. If you have not
written the word clearly or correctly, write it again.

5 CHECK what you learned.
Cover the word and write it. If you did not spell the word
correctly, practice these steps until you can write it correctly
every time.

Lesson Word Log
Look in the back of this book, starting on page
110. This is where you'll list the words that you
need to study from each lesson. Include words
you miss on the pretest and any other words
you aren't sure you can always spell correctly.

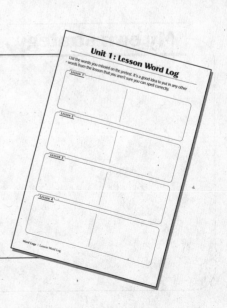

Spelling Strategies

Here are some helpful spelling strategies. Think about them as you come across words you don't know how to spell.

➤ **Say the word.** Then close your eyes, and picture the way it's spelled. Spell it silently, and then write it.

➤ **Think of ways** to spell the vowel sound in a word. Try different spellings until the word looks right. For example, does *bild* look right or does *build* look right?

➤ **Think about the rules** that tell what spelling changes to make before adding *-ed* and *-ing* or changing *y* to *i*.

➤ **Think of a rhyming word** to help you figure out how to spell another word.

➤ **Make up a silly sentence** or phrase if it helps you remember how to spell a word. For example—

> If you can't remember how to spell *reign,* try a sentence such as *Ron's elegant iguana got nervous.* If you put together the first letters of each word, you have *reign!*

My own strategy . . .

Proofreading Strategies

➤ **Proofread your work twice.** The first time, circle words you know are misspelled. Then go back and look for words that you are not sure about.

➤ **Read the words backward.** Start with the last word and end with the first word. That may sound funny, but it may help you notice words that are misspelled!

➤ **Look for homophones,** and make sure each word you've written makes sense.

➤ **Make a chart to keep track of your spelling errors.** Then you can see what kinds of mistakes you make and work to correct them.

My own strategy . . .

How to Make Your Personal Word Log

A Personal Word Log is your own word collection. It's a place where you can store words that are special to you—words you need to know for classes, words with unusual meanings, or just words that you think are interesting. How can you develop your Personal Word Log? Here are some tips.

➤ **Watch for** especially interesting or unusual words when you're reading. Jot them down, and then add them to your Log!

➤ **When you watch** television or listen to the radio, listen for any new words that you would like to save. The word might be used by a favorite entertainer. Maybe it's a word used during a news broadcast.

➤ **Include words** that you need to use when you write, especially words that are hard for you to spell.

➤ **Include words** you have trouble spelling or pronouncing.

➤ **Think about** technical words used in your school subjects— mathematics, social studies, science.

➤ **Before you write** a word in your Log, check the spelling. You might look up the word in a dictionary or a thesaurus or ask a classmate for help.

➤ **Here's a helpful hint:** Keep notes on your words. To help you remember the meaning of a word, write a definition, a synonym, or an antonym. You might also use the word in a sentence. Or, write anything you remember about the word that makes it interesting. Look at the sample on the next page.

WORD AND NOTES

serendipitous

Serendipitous has a dip in the middle.

Serendipitous means "finding something by accident."

While flipping through a library book, she made a serendipitous discovery—a five-dollar bill.

Personal Word Log

You'll find your own Personal Word Log in the back of the book, starting on page 116.

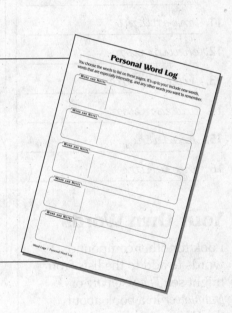

Lesson 1: Compound Words

Spelling Words

1. overnight
2. underwater
3. sailboat
4. life jackets
5. offshore
6. strawberry
7. daylight
8. seaweed
9. wildlife
10. grandparents
11. moonlight
12. chairperson
13. killer whale
14. watermelon
15. headache
16. typewriter

Your Own Words

Look for other compound words to add to the lists. You might see *Thanksgiving* or *Mayflower* in a book about the Pilgrims. You might use *earthquake* or *tidal wave* in a report about disasters.

17. _____
18. _____
19. _____
20. _____

Each Spelling Word is a compound word. Look at the words that make up each compound word.

Sort the Spelling Words into categories to help you remember them.

CLOSED
downfall

_____   _____
_____   _____
_____   _____
_____   _____
_____   _____
_____   _____

OPEN
tidal wave

_____   _____
_____   _____

➤ **Closed compound words are spelled without a space between the two words.**

➤ **Open compound words are spelled with a space between the two words.**

Lesson 1: Compound Words (continued)

SPELLING CLUES: Parts and Whole When you write, make sure you spell each part of a compound word correctly. Then decide if the compound word should be open or closed. Then recheck the spelling of each part of the compound word.

Look at the two possible spellings. Write the correct spelling of each word.

1. chair person   chairperson
2. typewriter   type writer
3. strawberry   straw berry
4. head ache   headache
5. wildlife   wild life
6. water melon   watermelon

PROOFREADING 7–11. Circle each incorrect compound word in the school newspaper article below. Then write the words correctly on the lines.

STUDENT SAILOR

Middle-school student Erica Murphy took a 22-foot sail boat 500 miles down the coast to visit her grand parents in San Diego. Erica sailed by day light and by moon light. She says the most thrilling part was being on the water over night.

FUN WITH WORDS Write Spelling Words to replace 12–16.

1. _____
2. _____
3. _____
4. _____
5. _____
6. _____
7. _____
8. _____
9. _____
10. _____
11. _____

12. _____
13. _____
14. _____
15. _____
16. _____

Lesson 2: Homophones

Spelling Words

1. real
2. missed
3. pain
4. tide
5. shoot
6. mist
7. birth
8. swayed
9. shown
10. tied
11. pane
12. shone
13. reel
14. berth
15. chute
16. suede

Each Spelling Word is half of a pair of homophones. Homophones are words that are pronounced the same but are spelled differently and have different meanings.

Sort the Spelling Words so that the homophones in each pair are together. Write each pair.

eight	ate

Most pairs of homophones begin with the same letter.

Your Own Words

Look for other homophones to add to the lists. You might see *eight* and *ate* in a math book. You might find *capitol* and *capital* in a social studies book.

17. _____
18. _____
19. _____
20. _____

Lesson 2: Homophones *(continued)*

SPELLING CLUES: Thinking About Meaning To choose the correct homophone, think about the meaning of the word and how it fits with the meaning of the entire sentence.

Write the homophone that correctly completes each sentence.

1. Cold air rushed in through the broken (pane, pain) of the kitchen window.
2. Amy felt a tug on the line and began to (real, reel) in a huge fish.
3. Beginners must be (shone, shown) how to do the job correctly.
4. Joe took an upper (berth, birth) in the train's sleeping compartment.

1. _____
2. _____
3. _____
4. _____

PROOFREADING 5–8. Read the diary entry. Circle the incorrect homophones, and write the correct homophones on the lines.

Dear Diary,
Today at the hospital I worked with Eddie.
Eddie hasn't spoken since berth. I can sense a
reel pane behind his blank expression. However,
after our session, I think his eyes shown a
little more brightly than before.

5. _____
6. _____
7. _____
8. _____

FUN WITH WORDS Replace 9–16 with Spelling Words. The words in each sentence should be homophones.

- The __9__ was high when we __10__ the boat to the dock.
- In this game, you try to __11__ the ball so that it comes down the __12__ with the highest number on it.
- Because it was hard to see in the __13__ , we __14__ our exit off the highway.
- The woman in the __15__ skirt could not be __16__ from making a long speech.

9. _____
10. _____
11. _____
12. _____
13. _____
14. _____
15. _____
16. _____

Lesson 3: Adding Endings to Words

Spelling Words

1. letting
2. following
3. cheating
4. labored
5. gathered
6. hammered
7. controlling
8. bothering
9. ruined
10. listening
11. studying
12. swallowed
13. permitting
14. carrying
15. compelled
16. groaned

Your Own Words

Look for other words in which the base word does or doesn't change. You might see *batted* or *stealing* in an article about baseball. You might find *taxed* or *rebelling* in a book about colonial America.

17. _____
18. _____
19. _____
20. _____

Each Spelling Word ends in *-ed* or *-ing*. Look at the base words and notice what happens when the endings are added.

Sort the Spelling Words into categories to help you remember them.

BASE WORD CHANGES
sitting / hopped

_____ _____
_____ _____

BASE WORD DOESN'T CHANGE
allowing / gained

_____ _____
_____ _____
_____ _____
_____ _____
_____ _____

Before adding an ending to words that have a short vowel sound followed by a single consonant, double the consonant.

Lesson 3: Adding Endings to Words *(continued)*

SPELLING CLUES: Comparing Spellings When you proofread, look for words that may be misspelled. Write each word the way you think it should be spelled. Then decide which spelling is correct.

Look at the two possible spellings. Write the spelling that looks correct. Use the Spelling Dictionary if you need help.

1. groanned   groaned
2. cheating   cheatting
3. controlling   controling
4. permiting   permitting
5. swallowed   swallowwed
6. gatherred   gathered

1. _____
2. _____
3. _____
4. _____
5. _____
6. _____

PROOFREADING 7–11. Proofread the letter to the author. Circle the misspelled words. Then write the words correctly on the lines.

> Dear Beverly Cleary,
>
> We are studing one of your books in class, and I felt compeled to write you. I want to be a writer, too. Would you mind leting me know how you get your ideas? Do you spend a lot of time listenning to young people? Are you always carring a notebook to write down ideas? Thank you.
>
> Sincerely,
> Scott Thomas

7. _____
8. _____
9. _____
10. _____
11. _____

FUN WITH WORDS Write Spelling Words to replace 12–16.

YOU LOOK UPSET. WHAT'S _12_ YOU?

WHY? THAT'S A NEAT SCULPTURE.

I _13_ OVER THIS GIFT FOR MY DAD IN SHOP CLASS. I _14_ NAILS UNTIL MY THUMBS WERE NUMB. NOW MY PRESENT IS _15_.

YEAH, BUT I WAS _16_ THE INSTRUCTIONS FOR MAKING A BIRDHOUSE.

12. _____
13. _____
14. _____
15. _____
16. _____

Lesson 4: Words from Spanish

Spelling Words

1. patio
2. rodeo
3. tornado
4. tomato
5. cafeteria
6. alligator
7. corral
8. vanilla
9. mosquito
10. stampede
11. guitar
12. coyote
13. jaguar
14. chili
15. cocoa
16. tortillas

Your Own Words

Look for other words from Spanish to add to the lists. You might find *pinto* or *bronco* in a book about horses. You might use *canyon* or *mesa* in a geography report.

17. _____
18. _____
19. _____
20. _____

Each Spelling Word comes from Spanish. Look at the words carefully.

Sort the Spelling Words into categories to help you remember them.

PLACES
plaza

_____
_____
_____

EVENTS
fiesta

_____
_____
_____

ANIMALS AND **OBJECTS**
burro

_____
_____
_____
_____
_____
_____

FOOD
taco

_____
_____
_____
_____
_____
_____

Many words that are Spanish in origin have become part of everyday speech in English.

Lesson 4: Words from Spanish *(continued)*

SPELLING CLUES: Mnemonics Think about a word that you have difficulty spelling. Verbalize a clue to help you remember how to spell the word. For example, to remember the correct spelling of the word *classical*, you might use this sentence: *I'd like to take a class in classical music.*

Write the correct spelling of each word. Then think of a mnemonic to help you remember how to spell the word.

1. corral, corale
2. tornado, tornadoe
3. tomato, tamato
4. musquito, mosquito
5. vanila, vanilla

PROOFREADING 6–10. Circle the misspelled words. Then write the words correctly on the lines.

CONCERT TONIGHT
Join the stampeed to hear
Cyote Clark and his Wild Dogs.
Appearing tonight in the school cafateria.
Free refreshments: Flour tortilas, and hot coco.

FUN WITH WORDS Write Spelling Words to replace 11–16.

FAUSTO'S SONG

My name is Fausto, and I know I'd go far

If only I could find a tuneful __11__ .

I'd sing about horses riding in the __12__ .

I'd sing about my grandmother, resting on her __13__ .

I'd sing about saving the rain forest's __14__ .

I'd sing about eating homemade __15__ from a jar.

I'd sing about an old __16__ living in the Everglades.

I'd sing and I'd sing until the sun fades.

1. _____
2. _____
3. _____
4. _____
5. _____
6. _____
7. _____
8. _____
9. _____
10. _____

11. _____
12. _____
13. _____
14. _____
15. _____
16. _____

Lesson 5: Music Words

Spelling Words

1. harp
2. composer
3. fiddle
4. trumpet
5. classical
6. conductor
7. concert
8. jazz
9. clarinet
10. banjo
11. bugle
12. harmony
13. pianist
14. performance
15. violin
16. rehearsal

Your Own Words

Look for other music words to add to the lists. You might find *drummer* or *solo* in a review of a rock concert. You might use *piano* or *jazz* in a report about a specific musician.

17. _____
18. _____
19. _____
20. _____

Each Spelling Word has something to do with music. Study the words carefully.

Sort the Spelling Words into categories to help you remember them.

INSTRUMENTS
drum

_____   _____

_____   _____

_____   _____

_____

MUSICAL TERMS
orchestra

_____

_____

_____

MUSICIANS
violinist

_____

_____

Some words are specialized—that is, they are used most frequently in certain fields of work or study.

➤ **Fields that may require a specialized vocabulary include music, science, medicine, mathematics, and computer science.**

First Course | *Spelling*

Lesson 5: Music Words (continued)

SPELLING CLUES: Checking Twice When you proofread, read once and circle words you know are misspelled. Then read again and look for other words that might be misspelled.

1–5. Read the list twice. Circle the five spelling errors. Then write the correct spelling.

banjoe	fidle	rehearsal
composer	violin	jaz
conductor	bugle	clarinet
harmeny	pianist	trumpit

PROOFREADING 6–11. Proofread the flyer twice. Circle the misspelled words. Then write the words correctly on the lines.

NOTICE

Special Consert of Clasical Music
Nadja Salerno-Sonnenberg
will play the volin
accompanied by her mother, a painist,
and by Cody Austin on the clairinet.
Performance Saturday at 8:00 P.M.
in the High School Auditorium

FUN WITH WORDS Write the Spelling Word that answers each riddle.

12. I wake the soldiers at dawn's first light,
     then play them "Taps," at the start of the night.
13. Play it once, play it twice.
     At me you'll play it till it sounds nice.
14. When a player plucks my strings,
     some folks imagine angels' wings.
15. Up in front, waving a stick,
     I tell the orchestra when to go slow, when to go quick.
16. Before the show starts, my work is done.
     Putting notes on paper is how I have fun.

1. _____
2. _____
3. _____
4. _____
5. _____

6. _____
7. _____
8. _____
9. _____
10. _____
11. _____

12. _____
13. _____
14. _____
15. _____
16. _____

Unit 1 Review
Practice Test: Part A

Read each group of phrases. Find the underlined word that is misspelled. Fill in the answer circle for that phrase.

EXAMPLE:

A writes <u>often</u>
B <u>successfull</u> business
C drive <u>carefully</u>
D <u>special</u> talent

1. A terrible <u>headache</u>
   B neck <u>pain</u>
   C day light <u>saving</u>
   D high <u>tide</u>

2. A three <u>life</u> jackets
   B incredible <u>killer</u> whale
   C hot <u>tortilas</u>
   D <u>vanilla</u> ice cream

3. A lone <u>coyote</u>
   B <u>wildlife</u> preserve
   C electric <u>typewriter</u>
   D accomplished <u>pianest</u>

4. A <u>missed</u> basket
   B <u>controling</u> the ship
   C caught <u>cheating</u>
   D steel <u>guitar</u>

5. A fishing <u>reel</u>
   B <u>groned</u> loudly
   C <u>listening</u> closely
   D swift <u>jaguar</u>

6. A <u>swallowed</u> hard
   B <u>suede</u> coat
   C <u>studying</u> often
   D upper <u>birth</u>

7. A ripe <u>strawberry</u>
   B red <u>tomato</u>
   C powerful <u>tornadoe</u>
   D juicy <u>watermelon</u>

8. A horse <u>stampeed</u>
   B fine <u>performance</u>
   C tied <u>tightly</u>
   D <u>mosquito</u> bite

9. A orchestra <u>conductor</u>
   B <u>following</u> orders
   C three-part <u>harmeny</u>
   D happy <u>grandparents</u>

10. A western <u>rodio</u>
    B <u>classical</u> musician
    C stringed <u>instrument</u>
    D <u>seaweed</u> floating

EXAMPLE

Ⓐ ●Ⓑ Ⓒ Ⓓ

ANSWERS

1 Ⓐ Ⓑ Ⓒ Ⓓ
2 Ⓐ Ⓑ Ⓒ Ⓓ
3 Ⓐ Ⓑ Ⓒ Ⓓ
4 Ⓐ Ⓑ Ⓒ Ⓓ
5 Ⓐ Ⓑ Ⓒ Ⓓ
6 Ⓐ Ⓑ Ⓒ Ⓓ
7 Ⓐ Ⓑ Ⓒ Ⓓ
8 Ⓐ Ⓑ Ⓒ Ⓓ
9 Ⓐ Ⓑ Ⓒ Ⓓ
10 Ⓐ Ⓑ Ⓒ Ⓓ

Unit 1 Review (continued)
Practice Test: Part B

Read each sentence. Fill in the letter of the correctly spelled word.

EXAMPLE: When do you think you will arrive _____?
  A hear   B here   C hier   D heare

1. I _____ my plane.
   A mist   B missed   C misst   D mised

2. The glass _____ in the kitchen is broken.
   A paine   B pain   C pane   D payne

3. Do you know how to swim _____?
   A underwater   C under water
   B underwatter   D underwaer

4. The family _____ together for a picnic.
   A gatherred   C gatherd
   B gatered   D gathered

5. I eat lunch in the school _____.
   A cafetiria   B cafateria   C cafeteria   D cafatiria

6. The light from the sun _____ brightly.
   A shoan   B shone   C shown   D shoen

7. He enjoys playing the _____ at all family gatherings.
   A fidle   B fidel   C fiddle   D fidal

8. The rain _____ our plans.
   A runed   B ruined   C riuned   D ruinned

9. The soloist played the _____ in the concert.
   A violin   B vilin   C vielin   D vylin

10. Have you ever eaten _____?
    A chilli   B chilly   C chile   D chili

EXAMPLE

Ⓐ ⓑ Ⓒ Ⓓ

ANSWERS

1 Ⓐ Ⓑ Ⓒ Ⓓ

2 Ⓐ Ⓑ Ⓒ Ⓓ

3 Ⓐ Ⓑ Ⓒ Ⓓ

4 Ⓐ Ⓑ Ⓒ Ⓓ

5 Ⓐ Ⓑ Ⓒ Ⓓ

6 Ⓐ Ⓑ Ⓒ Ⓓ

7 Ⓐ Ⓑ Ⓒ Ⓓ

8 Ⓐ Ⓑ Ⓒ Ⓓ

9 Ⓐ Ⓑ Ⓒ Ⓓ

10 Ⓐ Ⓑ Ⓒ Ⓓ

Unit 1 Review (continued)
Activities

What's in a Word?

◆ *banjo*

The word *banjo* comes from an African language—probably Kimbundu, a Bantu language. The word was brought to America by enslaved Africans.

cafeteria

The word *cafeteria* comes from a Spanish American word that originally meant "coffeehouse" or "coffee store." Eventually, it came to mean any self-service restaurant.

cowhands

We usually think of *cowhands* as people who care for cows, people who herd cows to green pastures and drive them to market. The tradition of the cowboy song actually began because cowboys sang their cows to sleep on the prairie. However, the word *cowboy* was first used during the Revolutionary War, and it meant people who stole cows and other property between British and American lines along the Hudson River. Surprising, isn't it?

◆ *corral*

The word *corral* comes from a word meaning "to run." This word was brought to the United States by Spanish-speaking cowboys. In Africa, the similar word *kraal* is used in the same way that we use *corral*, to describe a pen for animals. The word *kraal* comes from Portuguese, a language that is very closely related to Spanish. *Kraal* is an African word.

◆ This indicates a Unit Spelling Word.

Sailing Partners

Do this activity with a partner. Each of you should write a paragraph about some kind of boating adventure. Use five Spelling Words in your paragraph, but don't write down the Spelling Words. Instead, leave blanks where the Spelling Words should go. Exchange papers, and fill in the five Spelling Words that are missing from your partner's paragraph. Then exchange papers again, and check each other's spelling.

Picture Clues

Do this activity with a partner. Each partner should draw simple characters or scenes as clues to three Spelling Words. Trade drawings with your partner. Identify and write the correct Spelling Word under each of your partner's clues.

Proofreading Partners

Do this activity with a partner. Each of you should make a list of five Spelling Words that give you trouble or that you think are the most challenging to spell. Exchange lists. Each partner then writes a paragraph in which the other person's five words are misspelled. Then exchange papers, and proofread and correct each other's paragraphs. Be sure each Spelling Word is spelled correctly.

Homophone Fun

Think of a sentence in which you can use a pair of homophones that are Spelling Words. Write the sentence, but leave blanks for the homophones. Challenge a classmate to fill in the blanks with the correct Spelling Words.

Unit 1 Review *(continued)*
Activities

Team Charades

Do this activity with at least three people on each team. Divide the Spelling Words so that each team has half of them. Each team writes on a slip of paper a clue—a familiar phrase, a book title, a movie title, a common saying—for each of their words. Then all slips are given to the other team. One at a time, each team member draws a slip, takes one minute to plan, and then acts out the clue for his or her team. When the word is guessed and then spelled correctly, it's the other team's turn. Play continues until all clues have been acted out and guessed.

Spelling Duet

Do this activity with a partner. Write each Spelling Word on a slip of paper. Fold the slips and put them in a container or a pile. Take turns choosing a word and giving your partner as many one-word clues as necessary until he or she guesses the Spelling Word and spells it correctly. An example of a series of clues would be *bites, insect, tiny, itchy* (mosquito).

WHAT <u>IS</u> IN A WORD?

Start your own collection of word histories. Trace the development of at least two words from each Spelling Word list. Keep your collection in a separate notebook. Add to it not just Spelling Words but new and interesting words you come across in your reading.

What's in a Word?

eavesdrop

Originally, eavesdrops were drops of rain that fell from the eaves of a house. Later, to *eavesdrop* came to mean "to stand within the eaves of a house, or near its windows, to hear what people inside were saying." Now we use the word whenever we mean "to listen to what others are saying without their knowledge or permission."

eccentric

The word *eccentric* comes from a Greek word meaning "out of the center." It has come to mean "out of the ordinary" or "odd." Literature is full of eccentric characters. You may have met some in Lewis Carroll's *Alice's Adventures in Wonderland*. Charles Dickens also created many eccentric characters in such works as *A Christmas Carol* and *David Copperfield*.

◆ *killer whale*

A *killer whale* is actually a dolphin, a type of toothed whale. The scientific name for a killer whale is *Orcinus orca*. Killer whales were originally called "whale killers," because they prey on large fish, seals, and other whales. Then, for some reason, the two parts of the compound word were switched, leading to the name they are known by today.

◆ This indicates a Unit Spelling Word.

Lesson 7: Prefixes *en-* and *ex-*

Spelling Words

1. encourage
2. exit
3. enjoying
4. exchange
5. express
6. envelope
7. extend
8. excitement
9. exceed
10. explode
11. enthusiasm
12. enclose
13. expand
14. exclaim
15. exclude
16. excel

Your Own Words

Look for other words that begin with *en-* or *ex-* to add to the lists. You might see *exact* or *example* in a math book. You might use *exhort* or *encounter* when writing a detective story.

17. _____
18. _____
19. _____
20. _____

Each Spelling Word begins with the prefix *en-* or *ex-*. A prefix is a word part that is added to the beginning of a root that changes the root's meaning. Look at the beginning of each word to see how it is spelled.

Sort the Spelling Words by prefix to help you remember them.

EN-
enchant

_____ _____
_____ _____
_____

EX-
excess

_____ _____
_____ _____
_____ _____
_____

When the prefix *en-* or *ex-* is added to a root, the spelling of the root is not changed.

Lesson 7: Prefixes *en-* and *ex-* (continued)

SPELLING CLUES: Prefixes When you write a word beginning with *en-* or *ex-*, write the first syllable. Then concentrate on the spelling of the other syllable or syllables.

Read the sentences below. Determine what missing letters are needed to complete each Spelling Word. Then write each word.

1. The paper should ex_____ five pages.
2. Please ex_____ through the double doors.
3. She made an even ex_____.
4. Please en_____ a stamped envelope.
5. I heard him ex_____, "Oh!"
6. Please ex_____ the plot.

PROOFREADING 7–10. Circle the misspelled words. Then write the words correctly on the lines.

> Dear Marcus,
>
> If you are reading this letter, you must have opened the envelop. That's Step One. Step Two is reading these primitive squiggles. Good luck! I have to express my exsitment about your new stories! You added a new element: treachery! The situation keeps threatening to explohd. You're keeping me reading!
>
> Sincerely,
> Mick

FUN WITH WORDS Write Spelling Words to replace 11–16.

- People seemed to be __11__ themselves at the party.
- The coach made sure he did not __12__ anyone from the game.
- She had a lot of __13__ and school spirit.
- Please __14__ our thanks to the host and hostess.
- Some people seem to __15__ at everything they do.
- The teacher was able to __16__ her students to do their best.

1. _____
2. _____
3. _____
4. _____
5. _____
6. _____

7. _____
8. _____
9. _____
10. _____

11. _____
12. _____
13. _____
14. _____
15. _____
16. _____

Lesson 8: Prefixes *dis-* and *de-*

Spelling Words

1. disliked
2. discovered
3. decay
4. dispose
5. defeat
6. destroyed
7. decline
8. defects
9. disabled
10. disappeared
11. disappointment
12. dependent
13. deduction
14. disadvantages
15. disguised
16. dissolved

Your Own Words

Look for other words that begin with *dis-* or *de-*. You might use *decompose* or *disintegrate* in a science report. You might find *distinguished* or *declare* in a book about heroes.

17. _____
18. _____
19. _____
20. _____

Each Spelling Word begins with the prefix *dis-* or *de-*. Sometimes *dis-* or *de-* is a prefix added to a familiar word or root. Study each part of the word.

Sort the Spelling Words by prefix to help you remember them.

DIS-
disobey

DE-
debate

When the prefix *dis-* or *de-* is added to a root or to a familiar word, the spelling of the root or the base word is not changed.

Lesson 8: Prefixes *dis-* and *de-* (continued)

SPELLING CLUES: Prefixes When you write a word beginning with *dis-* or *de-*, write the first syllable. Then concentrate on the spelling of the other syllables.

Read these phrases. Determine what missing letters are needed to complete each Spelling Word. Write each word.

1. a dis_____ spaceship
2. a de_____ for our team
3. dis_____ by few
4. major design de_____
5. dis_____ of properly
6. dis_____ in water
7. name two dis_____

PROOFREADING 8–12. Circle the misspelled words. Then write the words correctly on the lines.

> **Oak Tree Gallery**
> **123 Oak St., Plains, GA 32323**
>
> Dear Ms. Kaminsky:
>   We regret to inform you that your painting <u>Golfo di Salerno</u> disapeered from our warehouse. You cannot imagine our disapointment. At first, we thought it had been destroied in the fire that damaged our main gallery, but a police detective believes a thief may have been disgysed as a firefighter. The police hope to recover it. The outcome is dependant on their ongoing work.

FUN WITH WORDS Write Spelling Words to replace 13–16.

1. _____
2. _____
3. _____
4. _____
5. _____
6. _____
7. _____

8. _____
9. _____
10. _____
11. _____
12. _____

13. _____
14. _____
15. _____
16. _____

Lesson 9: Places and People

Spelling Words

1. Japan
2. Africa
3. English
4. France
5. Spanish
6. Greek
7. England
8. African
9. French
10. Spain
11. Vietnam
12. Australia
13. Japanese
14. Greece
15. Australian
16. Vietnamese

Your Own Words

Look for other words that are the names of countries and continents and words that derive from them. You might use *Chile* and *Chilean* in a report about South America.

17. _____
18. _____
19. _____
20. _____

Each Spelling Word is the name of a country or a continent or a word that derives, or comes, from the country or continent name.

Sort the Spelling Words so that the countries and continents are all in one column and the words that come from them are in the other column. Example words have been given.

Canada	Canadian

Words that come from the names of countries and continents are formed in many different ways.

➤ **The word may take the ending -*ese*, -*ish*, or -*an*; or there may be an internal change in the word, as in *France/French*.**

➤ **If an ending is added, it may be necessary to drop a final vowel; for example, *Africa* + *an* = *African*.**

➤ **Other changes may occur to the word, as in *Spain/Spanish*.**

Lesson 9: Places and People (continued)

Spelling Clues: Comparing Spellings When you proofread, look for words that may be misspelled. Write each word the way you think it should be spelled. Then decide which spelling is correct. Remember to capitalize proper nouns and adjectives.

Look at the three possible spellings for each Spelling Word. Write the spelling that looks correct.

1. Spane   Spain   Spian
2. Japaneese   Japannese   Japanese
3. Greece   Greese   Grese
4. Vietnamese   Vietnameze   Vietnammese

PROOFREADING 5–11. Alicia has to explain in writing why she would like to take Advanced Placement French in high school. Help her proofread her rough draft. Circle the misspelled words. Then write the words correctly on the lines.

My parents are in the military, so we move a lot. My first language is Englesh, but I am almost as fluent in several other languages. Our first assignment was in France. It lasted two years, and I became quite fluent in French. After that we lived in South Afreca, and we traveled a lot. Swahili wasn't hard for me since Mom had been teaching it to me since I was a baby, but some of the other Africcan languages were tricky. Our next stop was Vietenam, where I again spoke Frenche. In Madrid, I understood the Spanesh I heard after about six months. I would like to improve my French before we move to Austrailia. I hope to study native languages there.

FUN WITH WORDS Write the Spelling Word that goes with each clue.

12. People who were the first Olympians
13. Where you can see the Eiffel Tower and eat a croissant
14. Where formal dress can be a kimono
15. A person who lives "down under"
16. Where Winnie-the-Pooh and Sherlock Holmes live

1. _____
2. _____
3. _____
4. _____

5. _____
6. _____
7. _____
8. _____
9. _____
10. _____
11. _____

12. _____
13. _____
14. _____
15. _____
16. _____

Lesson 10: Prefix *ad-*

Spelling Words

1. arrest _____
2. approve _____
3. accent _____
4. arrived _____
5. arrange _____
6. accommodate _____
7. announced _____
8. approaching _____
9. accepted _____
10. appoint _____
11. accompanying _____
12. array _____
13. arrangements _____
14. accomplish _____
15. accelerate _____
16. annoy _____

Your Own Words

Look for other words with these beginnings. You might find *accentuate* in a book about public speaking. You might include *arraignment* or *appalled* in a comic book you create.

17. _____
18. _____
19. _____
20. _____

Each Spelling Word includes a beginning that is a form of the prefix *ad-*. The spelling of the prefix changes when it is added to a root starting with *c, n, p,* or *r*. Look at the beginning of each word to see how it is spelled.

Sort the Spelling Words by the way they begin.

<u>accu</u>mulation
_____
_____
_____
_____
_____

<u>arr</u>ival
_____
_____
_____
_____
_____

<u>ann</u>ul
_____
_____
_____

<u>app</u>earing
_____
_____
_____

The prefix *ad-* changes when it is added to roots beginning with the letters *c, n, p,* or *r*. The *d* in the prefix changes to the first letter of the root.

First Course | *Spelling*

Lesson 10: Prefix *ad-* (continued)

SPELLING CLUES: Prefixes When you write a word using one of the prefixes in this lesson, think about the root. Then use the prefix that ends with the same letter that begins the root.

Add a prefix that means "to" to each of the roots below. Add necessary suffixes as well. Write the Spelling Word.

1. Could Yasha _____complish anything useful?
2. Yasha worried that his music might _____noy others.
3. In the city, the _____cent was on artistic endeavor.
4. A flute player _____cept_____ him as a student.
5. He helped Yasha _____celerate his training.
6. Soon Yasha's music was beautiful enough to _____rest the attention of the king.
7. The king decided to _____point Yasha a court musician.

1. _____
2. _____
3. _____
4. _____
5. _____
6. _____
7. _____

PROOFREADING 8–12. Circle the misspelled words. Then write the words correctly on the lines.

My Honored Father,
   I told the king that your seventieth birthday was aproaching, and he said he would aprove a short absence so I may visit you. The king is sending an erray of gems and finery. Thus, three guards are accompaning me. I hope it will not be hard for you to arange places for them to stay. I look forward to our visit.

                   Your loving son,
                   Yasha

8. _____
9. _____
10. _____
11. _____
12. _____

FUN WITH WORDS Write Spelling Words to replace 13–16.

I HOPE WE 13 ON TIME.

BUT YOU CANNOT BE THE CLASSICAL TRIO WE 14 IN OUR INVITATIONS!

THEY'RE REALLY SORRY, BUT THEY GOT SNOWED IN.

I THINK WE CAN 15 YOU. THEY FAXED US ALL THEIR MUSICAL 16.

13. _____
14. _____
15. _____
16. _____

Lesson 11: Adjective Suffixes

Spelling Words

1. backward
2. foolish
3. handsome
4. lonesome
5. selfish
6. marine
7. greenish
8. awkward
9. wholesome
10. grayish
11. childish
12. masculine
13. feminine
14. reddish
15. genuine
16. awesome

Your Own Words

Look for other words that end with -some, -ish, ine, and -ward. You might find *Scottish* or *northward* in a geography book. You might write *meddlesome* or *equine* in a story about the Wild West.

17. _____
18. _____
19. _____
20. _____

Each Spelling Word ends with a suffix. A suffix is a word part that is added to the end of a word or root. Look at the end of each word to see how it is spelled.

Sort the Spelling Words by suffixes to help you remember them.

smallish
_____
_____
_____
_____
_____

clandestine
_____
_____
_____
_____

southward
_____
_____

quarrelsome
_____
_____
_____
_____

Some suffixes indicate a word's part of speech.

➤ When the suffixes, -*some, -ish, -ine,* and -*ward* are added to words or roots, the words usually become adjectives.

➤ To spell a word with one of these suffixes, spell the root first and then add the suffix.

Lesson 11: Adjective Suffixes *(continued)*

SPELLING CLUES: Checking Twice When you proofread, read once and circle words you know are misspelled. Then read again and look for other words that might be misspelled.

1–7. Proofread the list twice. Circle the seven misspelled words. Then write the correct spelling of each Spelling Word.

back ward	winsome	abolish
languish	foolish	femnine
genuine	graish	marene
hansome	greenesh	masculin

1. _____
2. _____
3. _____
4. _____
5. _____
6. _____
7. _____

PROOFREADING 8–11. Proofread the paragraph below. Circle the misspelled words. Then write the words correctly on the lines.

> Sonja sighed as she pulled weeds from the redish Georgia soil. Her childesh dream of owning the mansion was as likely as finding fish on Mars. She felt folish when she remembered it. Now that she was the gardener, she could be at the mansion as much as she liked, without feeling ackwerd.

8. _____
9. _____
10. _____
11. _____

FUN WITH WORDS Write Spelling Words to replace 12–16.

THAT'S AN __12__ SIGHT.

THESE KIDS WERE GETTIN' __13__, SO I LASSOED 'EM SOME KITTENS TO PLAY WITH.

BUT THOSE ARE __14__ BENGAL TIGERS, BILL!

NOW DON'T GO FRETTIN' YOURSELF. OLE BILL DOESN'T LIKE TO BE __15__ WHEN __16__ FUN IS INVOLVED. THERE'S ONE FOR YOU TO RIDE, TOO.

12. _____
13. _____
14. _____
15. _____
16. _____

Lesson 12: Spelling and Pronunciation

Spelling Words

1. February
2. separate
3. different
4. library
5. temperature
6. strength
7. length
8. vegetable
9. arctic
10. twelfth
11. probably
12. jewelry
13. literature
14. boundary
15. reference
16. beverage

Your Own Words

Look for other words commonly misspelled because they are hard to pronounce. You might find *traveler* or *caterpillar* in a nature book. You might find *governor* or *comfortable* in a social studies book.

17. _____
18. _____
19. _____
20. _____

Each Spelling Word is sometimes pronounced differently from how it is spelled. That is because all the sounds in these words are not always said. Sometimes people misspell words because they don't pronounce each sound. Sometimes, however, people misspell words because the correct pronunciation interferes with the correct spelling. In the word *business,* the vowel sound is often omitted. In the word *paraphernalia,* a consonant sound may be omitted.

Say each Spelling Word aloud. Then sort them according to the letter often omitted in speech. Example words have been given.

OMITTED CONSONANTS
surprise

_____
_____
_____

OMITTED VOWELS
listener   **stationary**

_____   _____
_____   _____
_____   _____
_____   _____

Sometimes in speech, certain sounds are omitted. To spell a word correctly, keep in mind the pronunciation.

Lesson 12: Spelling and Pronunciation *(continued)*

SPELLING CLUES: Commonly Misspelled Words Some words are difficult to spell because they are long and unfamiliar. Other words may seem difficult to spell because they are pronounced incorrectly. Spelling words by syllables can help you spell words correctly.

Read each word below. Decide which letters are missing. Then spell the word by syllables. Write the Spelling Word correctly.

1. diffrent
2. lenth
3. vegtable
4. boundry
5. strenth
6. bevrage

PROOFREADING 7–12. Circle the misspelled words in the purchase order below. Then write the words correctly on the lines.

TO: Valley of the Sun Book Supply
FROM: Desert Circle Public Libary
Please send us these volumes by the twelfth of February.
Refrence section:
    Title: *A Beginner's Book of Vegetable Gardening*
    Title: *Native American Jewlry*
Literture section:
    Title: *Operation Artic*
    Title: *A Seprate Peace*

---

1. _____
2. _____
3. _____
4. _____
5. _____
6. _____

7. _____
8. _____
9. _____
10. _____
11. _____
12. _____

FUN WITH WORDS Write Spelling Words to replace 13–16.

THIS IS THE _13_ ONE OF THESE BIRDS WE'VE SEEN. THEY _14_ ARE HOT AND HUNGRY, TOO.

HOT? THE _15_ HAS JUST DROPPED 60 DEGREES!

AFTER ALL, IT IS _16_ !

13. _____
14. _____
15. _____
16. _____

Unit 2 Review
Practice Test: Part A

Read each sentence. Mark the circle to tell whether the underlined word is spelled correctly or incorrectly.

EXAMPLE: Hang the <u>pictcher</u> straight.

1. Do not <u>excede</u> the speed limit.
   correct   incorrect

2. He was <u>accepted</u> to music school.
   correct   incorrect

3. The fence will <u>encloze</u> the yard.
   correct   incorrect

4. The shortest month is <u>Febuary</u>.
   correct   incorrect

5. The purse <u>disappered</u> from the table.
   correct   incorrect

6. He was <u>disguised</u> for the party.
   correct   incorrect

7. I am taking lessons in <u>Japaneese</u>.
   correct   incorrect

8. The hotel can <u>accomodate</u> more than 300 guests.
   correct   incorrect

9. Is <u>Spanish</u> spoken in South America?
   correct   incorrect

10. He acted in a <u>childesh</u> manner.
    correct   incorrect

EXAMPLE
Correct   Incorrect

ANSWERS

1 ◯ ◯
2 ◯ ◯
3 ◯ ◯
4 ◯ ◯
5 ◯ ◯
6 ◯ ◯
7 ◯ ◯
8 ◯ ◯
9 ◯ ◯
10 ◯ ◯

First Course | *Spelling*

Unit 2 Review (continued)
Practice Test: Part B

Read each sentence. Fill in the letter of the correctly spelled word.

EXAMPLE: The entire proposal sounds _____.
A abserd   B absird   C absurd   D adsurd

1. Many of the things she did seemed to _____ me.
A annoye   B annoy   C annoi   D anoy

2. The new girl in my _____ class speaks with a slight accent.
A English   B Englesh   C english   D Englsh

3. Everyone seemed to be _____ the play.
A enjoing   B engoying   C enjoying   D injoying

4. Her actions seemed to be very _____.
A foolish   B folish   C fulish   D fulesh

5. When I go scuba diving, I like to study the _____ life.
A merine   B marene   C marean   D marine

6. The plants in the rain forest are being _____.
A distroyed   C destroyed
B destroied   D desstroyed

7. To be sure you measure the exact _____ of the frame, use a ruler.
A lenth   B lengh   C length   D lingh

8. We visited _____ last year.
A Greaze   B Greece   C Greese   D Grease

9. He was the _____ person in line for concert tickets.
A twelfth   B twelth   C twelf   D twelph

10. Did they _____ the person who broke into your home?
A arest   B areste   C arress   D arrest

EXAMPLE
Ⓐ Ⓑ ⬤C Ⓓ

ANSWERS
1 Ⓐ Ⓑ Ⓒ Ⓓ
2 Ⓐ Ⓑ Ⓒ Ⓓ
3 Ⓐ Ⓑ Ⓒ Ⓓ
4 Ⓐ Ⓑ Ⓒ Ⓓ
5 Ⓐ Ⓑ Ⓒ Ⓓ
6 Ⓐ Ⓑ Ⓒ Ⓓ
7 Ⓐ Ⓑ Ⓒ Ⓓ
8 Ⓐ Ⓑ Ⓒ Ⓓ
9 Ⓐ Ⓑ Ⓒ Ⓓ
10 Ⓐ Ⓑ Ⓒ Ⓓ

Unit 2 Review (continued)
Activities

What's in a Word?

◆ *arctic*

Arctic is sometimes mispronounced as if the word were "artic," without a *c*. *Arctic* comes from *arktos*, an ancient word meaning "the bear." The Great Bear is a group of stars thought to form the shape of a bear. These stars appear in the northern sky and thus are associated with the far northern regions of the earth.

befriend / befuddle

The prefix *be-* has several meanings. In some words such as *befriend*, it means "treat as." In *befuddle*, it means "thoroughly." Today, however, many of the words with the prefix *be-* are used only to set a certain mood or tone in writing. Instead of writing "He was a friend to her," you might say "He befriended her." Instead of writing "See the bright object in the sky," you might say "Behold the bright object in the sky." Instead of writing "She was confused," you might say "She was befuddled." Use this to your advantage. When you write a play or story, try using a "*be*-something" word and see if it sets a particular mood or tone.

◆ This indicates a Unit Spelling Word.

Prefixes That Describe Where

English uses many prefixes that describe where. *De-* means "from" or "down." To *decay* is "to fall *from* goodness or soundness; to rot." To *deport* is "to send *from* a place." *Ex-* means "out." To *explode* is "to burst *outward*." All the prefixes in the list describe where.

a-	=	on	*mid-*	=	middle
ab-	=	from	*para-*	=	beside
by-	=	near, aside	*peri-*	=	around
circum-	=	through, across	*retro-*	=	back
epi-	=	upon	*sub-*	=	under
extra-	=	outside	*super-*	=	over
hypo-	=	under	*tele-*	=	distant
im- (in-)	=	into	*trans-*	=	across
intra-	=	within			

Work with a partner to see how many words you can come up with, using each prefix from the list. Compare your list with that of another pair of students. Combine your lists, and add up the total.

ENDURANCE SPELLING

With a partner, play a game to review the Spelling Words. Read the words, and ask your partner to spell each word aloud as quickly as possible. Then switch roles. Which of you can *endure* the pressure and spell all the words correctly?

Spelling Crossword

Review the Spelling Words, and choose at least seven words to use in a crossword puzzle. Plan where each word will fit in your puzzle, remembering that each word should share a letter with at least one other word. Following your plan, draw a box for every letter of each word. Add as many other words as you like to your crossword. Then write clues for each word. Ask a classmate to solve your puzzle.

Unit 2 Review (continued)
Activities

Fantastic Folks

Play this game with a group of four. Divide the Spelling Words by the number of people in the group so that each person has four Spelling Words. Each person should create a fictitious person's name and habits, beginning with each assigned Spelling Word. Try to include alliteration and rhyme (the sillier the better). For example, *Backward Bill buried ten more men at Boot Hill or Selfish Selina samples shellfish at Salina's Marina*. Share your sayings with your group. Then choose three favorites, write them down, and add them to a class collection.

Proofreading Partners

Do this activity with a partner. Each of you should make a list of five Spelling Words that give you trouble or the five words you consider the most challenging in general. Exchange lists. Each partner should write a paragraph on any topic you choose. Use your partner's five Spelling Words in your paragraph, but misspell them. Then exchange papers, and proofread and correct each other's paragraphs. Be sure each Spelling Word is spelled correctly.

SUFFIX SCRAMBLE

Work with a partner. Write the Spelling Words on cards. Take turns choosing a card. Give each other a clue about the word on the card you have chosen. For example, if you choose the word *majority*, you could say, "This word describes a group and ends in –*ity*." Each correct answer is worth one point.

clamber

The word *clamber* is a colorful word that almost sounds like what it means, which is "to climb using both hands and feet, in a clumsy manner." It comes from Middle English. It is like the German word *klammern* in the phrase *sich klammern*, which means "to hook oneself on or cling firmly." *Clamber* is often used to describe how people get to the top of something like a class, a business, or a field of artistic endeavor.

◆ February / October

February comes from a Latin word which means "to purify by sacrifice." Thus, *February* was the month of purification. *October* comes from the Latin word, *octo*, meaning "eight," because it was the eighth month of the original Roman year.

◆ marine

The word *marine* means "having to do with the ocean." A *Marine* is a member of one of the four branches of the United States armed forces. Today we may think of the United States *Marine* Corps as operating more on land than at sea. However, when the first *marines* went into service in the British navy in the 1600s, they were soldiers who served on board a ship to protect the sailors.

◆ This indicates a Unit Spelling Word.

Lesson 14: Noun Suffixes

Spelling Words

1. bakery
2. victory
3. documentary
4. factory
5. machinery
6. discovery
7. nursery
8. dictionary
9. century
10. injury
11. missionary
12. territory
13. scenery
14. revolutionary
15. treasury
16. luxury

Your Own Words

Look for other words with these endings. You might find *adversary* and *misery* in an article about the Klondike gold rush. You might find *depository* and *usury* in an article about money.

17. _____
18. _____
19. _____
20. _____

Each Spelling Word ends with a suffix. When the suffixes *-ary*, *-ory*, *-ery*, and *-ury* are added to words, nouns are formed.

Sort the Spelling Words by suffix to help you remember them. Add your own category and example word for the fourth category as you are sorting.

-ARY
infirmary

_____
_____
_____

-ERY
pottery

_____
_____
_____

-ORY
laboratory

_____
_____
_____

_____
_____
_____

The suffixes *-ary*, *-ory*, *-ery*, and *-ury* are added to words to form nouns.

➤ When the suffix *-ary* is added to a root word, the spelling of the root word usually does not change.

➤ When the suffix *-ery*, *-ory*, or *-ury* is added to a root word, the spelling of the root word often changes in some way.

Lesson 14: Noun Suffixes (continued)

SPELLING CLUES: Comparing Spellings When you proofread, think about how you have seen the word written before. Does the word look right when you write it on paper?

Look at the three possible spellings for each Spelling Word. Write the spelling that looks correct. Use the Spelling Dictionary if you need help.

1. century   centery   centurey
2. dictonary   dictionery   dictionary
3. revolutionry   revolutionary revolutionery
4. injury   injurey   ingiry
5. mishinery   missinary   missionary
6. senery   scenery   seenery

1. _____
2. _____
3. _____
4. _____
5. _____
6. _____

PROOFREADING 7–12. Proofread this diary entry. Circle the misspelled words. Then write the words correctly on the lines.

> Dear Diary,
> I've been searching for gold in this freezing teritory for months. Sometimes I think I'll never add a nickel's worth of money to my treasurey. Victorry always seems near, but it is never quite within my grasp.
>   A simple thing like a warm bed seems like an impossible luxery. The idea of a tasty roll from a backery makes my mouth water. The documentery I saw long ago about gold mining was the beginning of my misery.

7. _____
8. _____
9. _____
10. _____
11. _____
12. _____

FUN WITH WORDS Write Spelling Words to replace 13–16.

WHAT'S MY JOB?

I WORK IN A 13, WHERE I HELP MAKE MINING EQUIPMENT.

I WORK IN A FACTORY REPAIRING HEAVY 14.

THE LABORATORY I WORK IN HAS MADE AN IMPORTANT 15.

I WORK IN A 16, AND MY COMPANY SENDS FLOWERS, SEEDS, AND BULBS ALL OVER THE WORLD.

13. _____
14. _____
15. _____
16. _____

Lesson 15: Consonant and Syllable Patterns

Spelling Words

1. gallery
2. tomorrow
3. attitude
4. hurricane
5. barrier
6. corridor
7. umbrella
8. buffalo
9. gorilla
10. pinnacle
11. syllable
12. tobacco
13. massacre
14. opossum
15. moccasins
16. cinnamon

Your Own Words

Look for other words that follow these patterns to add to the lists. You might find *slippery* and *beginning* in a story about mountain climbing.

17. _____
18. _____
19. _____
20. _____

Each Spelling Word has its own syllable pattern. Look at each word. Notice which syllables are accented in relation to the vowel and consonant pattern.

Sort the Spelling Words by pattern to help you remember them.

ACCENT ON THE FIRST SYLLABLE
difficult

_____ _____

_____ _____

_____ _____

_____

ACCENT ON THE SECOND SYLLABLE
im**pos**sible

_____ _____

_____ _____

_____

If a word has a double consonant, the accent often falls on the syllable that goes with the first of the double consonants.

Lesson 15: Consonant and Syllable Patterns (continued)

SPELLING CLUES: Reading Aloud When you are writing or proofreading, try saying aloud the word you are having trouble with. Listen to the sounds in the word, and think about the letters that usually spell those sounds.

Read the three possible spellings aloud. Write the correct spelling of each Spelling Word.

1. massacre   masacre   masacker
2. sylable   syllable   silable
3. tobacko   tobbaco   tobacco
4. bufallo   buffalo   bufalow
5. unbrella   umbrella   umbrela
6. gorilla   gorrila   gorila

PROOFREADING 7–12. Proofread this newspaper report. Circle the misspelled words. Then write the words correctly on the lines.

MARCH   **THE NEWSPAPER**   25¢

A young camper identified as Melissa Devick was stranded near the pinacle of Mount Stanley yesterday. Ms. Devick's mocassins made it difficult for her to walk down the mountain. When she was rescued, her only remaining food was some cinammon cookies. Ms. Devick maintained a positive atitude. "I was in a huriccane last year," she said. "Starting tomorow, I think I'll stay home."

FUN WITH WORDS Look at the picture. Then write Spelling Words to replace 13–16.

1. _____
2. _____
3. _____
4. _____
5. _____
6. _____
7. _____
8. _____
9. _____
10. _____
11. _____
12. _____

13. _____
14. _____
15. _____
16. _____

Lesson 16: Related Words

Spelling Words

1. population
2. regular
3. circles
4. popular
5. muscular
6. triangle
7. muscle
8. circular
9. regulation
10. particles
11. particular
12. rectangle
13. vehicles
14. rectangular
15. triangular
16. vehicular

Your Own Words

Look for other words that follow this pattern. You might find *granular* or *granulation* in a book about the Egyptian or the Mayan pyramids. You might use *molecule* or *molecular* in a science report.

17. _____
18. _____
19. _____
20. _____

Each Spelling Word is one of a pair of words that is related through a common root word. In each pair, one word ends in *-ar* or *-le* (*-les*). The other word in each pair ends in *-ation* or *-ular*.

Sort the Spelling Words by pattern to help you remember them.

-AR TO -ATION

tab<u>ular</u>   tabul<u>ation</u>

_____   _____

_____   _____

-LE (-LES) TO -ULAR

sing<u>le</u>   sing<u>ular</u>

_____   _____

_____   _____

_____   _____

_____   _____

34

Lesson 16: Related Words (continued)

SPELLING CLUES: Word Shapes Sometimes, thinking about the shape of a word can help you remember the correct spelling. Is the whole word long and flat? Does a letter at the beginning of the word drop below the line? Do two letters at the end rise above the others? Keep these shape clues in mind when you write.

Look at each shape. Write the Spelling Word that fits each shape.

1. [shape]   2. [shape]   3. [shape]

4. [shape]   5. [shape]   6. [shape]

1. _____

2. _____

3. _____

4. _____

5. _____

6. _____

PROOFREADING 7–12. Proofread this paragraph. Circle the misspelled words. Then write the words correctly on the lines.

Gabriella and Charlie took two separate vehickles to the pyramids. They followed the reguler route to the ruins. Along the way, Gabriella was distracted by one particuliar sound. It sounded like the song of a populer bird in the animal park near her home. She stopped her car in a rectangyular clearing in the rain forest. After walking around in circules for a while, she finally saw the bird that was making the sound.

7. _____

8. _____

9. _____

10. _____

11. _____

12. _____

FUN WITH WORDS Read the rhymes. Write the Spelling Word that tells who or what is talking.

13. You use me when you lift heavy things.
    I am in your arms and in birds' wings.

14. I have four sides—two short and two long.
    If you say "square," then you will be wrong.

15. The number of my sides is three.
    What do you think I could be?

16. I am another word for "rule."
    Don't break me! That wouldn't be cool.

13. _____

14. _____

15. _____

16. _____

Lesson 17: Latin Roots

Spelling Words

1. judges
2. fortune
3. doubt
4. doubtless
5. doubtful
6. specialist
7. misfortune
8. fortunate
9. unfortunate
10. especially
11. specific
12. specifications
13. judicial
14. judgment
15. prejudice
16. undoubtedly

Your Own Words

Look for other words with these Latin roots to add to the lists. You might find *specifically* and *misjudge* in a story describing underwater life. You might find *fortuitous* and *dubious* in a story about treasure hunting.

17. _____
18. _____
19. _____
20. _____

Each Spelling Word has a Latin root. Study the words, and look for the Latin root in each word.

Sort the Spelling Words into four groups according to their Latin roots.

**-DUB-
-DOUBT-
doubted**
_____
_____
_____
_____

**-FORS-
-FORT-
fortunately**
_____
_____
_____
_____

**-JUD-
-JUDG-
judged**
_____
_____
_____
_____

**-SPEC-
specialize**
_____
_____
_____
_____

Knowing the meanings of Latin roots can help you understand many words in English. Some meanings of these Latin roots are

➤ *-dub-*: "uncertain"

➤ *-jud-*: "to judge"

➤ *-fors-*: "chance"

➤ *-spec-*: "to look" or "individual," "particular."

First Course | *Spelling*

Lesson 17: Latin Roots *(continued)*

SPELLING CLUES: Checking the Base Word or the Root
When you write a word with a suffix or a prefix, think about the spelling of
the base word or the root. Be sure to spell it correctly. Then make any spelling
changes required by the addition of the prefix or the suffix.

Compare the two spellings of each Spelling Word. Write
the correct spelling.

1. prejuice   prejudice   4. specialist   speccialist
2. especially   espesially   5. fortunate   fourtunate
3. doutful   doubtful   6. undoutly   undoubtedly

PROOFREADING 7–12. Proofread this note. Circle the
misspelled words. Then write the words correctly on
the lines.

> Dear Aunt Marguerite,
>   No dout you have been wondering what I've
> been doing on this trip. Well, I have had the good
> fourtune to go diving in these tropical waters. I
> received some very spcefic directions about how to
> use the diving equipment. I was careful because
> I had heard about an unfotunate accident that
> happened last week. It was one poor diver's
> misforchune to nearly run out of air. I used good
> jujdment, and I had a very successful dive. I'll tell
> you about it when I get home.
>
>   Love,
>   Manuel

FUN WITH WORDS Write Spelling Words to replace 13–16.

THE OPINION OF THREE 13 WAS NEEDED TO ESTABLISH THE VALUE OF THE OLD COIN.

THE COIN SEEMS TO FIT ALL THE 14 FOR A COIN OF GREAT HISTORIC VALUE.

IT IS THE FINDING OF THIS 15 COMMITTEE THAT THE COIN IS AUTHENTIC.

16 THE REST OF THE COINS ARE REAL, TOO. GRANDPA WOULD BE AMAZED!

1. _____
2. _____
3. _____
4. _____
5. _____
6. _____

7. _____
8. _____
9. _____
10. _____
11. _____
12. _____
13. _____
14. _____
15. _____
16. _____

Lesson 18: Verb Suffixes

Spelling Words

1. celebrate
2. realize
3. advertise
4. analyze
5. organize
6. cooperate
7. congratulate
8. exercise
9. calculate
10. illustrate
11. recognize
12. compromise
13. memorize
14. paralyze
15. criticize
16. inaugurate

Your Own Words

Look for other words with these suffixes to add to the lists. You might find *initiate* and *capitalize* in a business book. You might use *animate* in a story about cartoons.

17. _____
18. _____
19. _____
20. _____

Each Spelling Word ends with a suffix. When the suffixes *-ate*, *-ize*, *-yze*, and *-ise* are added to words, verbs are formed. Words ending in *-yze* and *-ise* are rare.

Sort the words in a way that will help you remember them. Categories have been given for two groups. Fill in the category heads for the other two groups as you are sorting.

-ATE
activate
_____
_____
_____
_____
_____

-IZE
standardize
_____
_____
_____
_____
_____

_____
_____

_____
_____

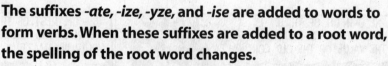

The suffixes *-ate*, *-ize*, *-yze*, and *-ise* are added to words to form verbs. When these suffixes are added to a root word, the spelling of the root word changes.

Lesson 18: Verb Suffixes (continued)

SPELLING CLUES: Visualizing Words When you are learning to spell a difficult word, study it carefully. Think about the patterns of the letters or the shapes certain letters in the word make. Then try to visualize the patterns or shapes. Try to see the written word in your mind.

Look at the two possible spellings. Write the correct spelling of each Spelling Word.

1. compromise   compromize
2. analize   analyze
3. cooperate   coperate
4. inaugurate   inauggurate
5. organize   organyze
6. recognize   recognyze

PROOFREADING 7–12. Circle the misspelled words. Then write the words correctly on the lines.

When Felipe got up to bat, he began to relize that he was afraid of failing. In fact, the fear he had was just about strong enough to paralise him. He was afraid that the coach would critisize everything he did. He had tried to memerize everything the coach had said. Now he tried to calcullate the speed at which the ball was moving. When he finally did hit the ball, he felt sure that everyone would congradulat him on overcoming his fear.

FUN WITH WORDS Write Spelling Words to replace 13–16.

13 _____   14 _____

15 _____   16 _____

1. _____
2. _____
3. _____
4. _____
5. _____
6. _____
7. _____
8. _____
9. _____
10. _____
11. _____
12. _____

13. _____
14. _____
15. _____
16. _____

Unit 3 Review
Practice Test: Part A

Read the possible spellings for each word. Mark the letter of the correctly spelled word.

EXAMPLE:

A cocoanut   C cokonut
B coconut   D coaconut

1. A dictionery   C dictionury
   B dictionary   D dicshunary

2. A especially   C especally
   B especialy   D ispecially

3. A ingery   C injery
   B ingury   D injury

4. A cinamon   C cinnamon
   B cinnamum   D cinnemon

5. A critisize   C criticyze
   B criticise   D criticize

6. A tommorrow   C tomorow
   B tomorrow   D tommorow

7. A prejudice   C predjudice
   B perjudice   D prejudise

8. A population   C popullation
   B poppulation   D populition

9. A compomise   C compromise
   B compromize   D compromyze

10. A musscle   C mussal
    B muskle   D muscle

EXAMPLE

(A) (B) (C) (D)

ANSWERS

1 (A) (B) (C) (D)

2 (A) (B) (C) (D)

3 (A) (B) (C) (D)

4 (A) (B) (C) (D)

5 (A) (B) (C) (D)

6 (A) (B) (C) (D)

7 (A) (B) (C) (D)

8 (A) (B) (C) (D)

9 (A) (B) (C) (D)

10 (A) (B) (C) (D)

Unit 3 Review (continued)
Practice Test: Part B

Find the correctly spelled word to complete each phrase.
Mark the answer.

EXAMPLE: _____ grateful
A extremly
B extreamly
C extremely
D extremele

1. important _____
A dicovery
B discovary
C descovery
D discovery

2. _____ orders
A specific
B speciffic
C spicific
D spesific

3. tiny _____
A partickles
B partikles
C particls
D particles

4. full of _____
A dout
B doute
C doubt
D dowbt

5. using good _____
A judgmant
B judgment
C judjment
D judjmant

6. wish to _____
A congradulate
B congratullate
C congratulate
D congratulait

7. _____ the text
A memorize
B memorise
C memarize
D memoraise

8. _____ a book
A ilustrate
B illustrait
C illistrate
D illustrate

9. herd of _____
A bufallo
B bufalow
C buffalo
D bufalo

10. unknown _____
A territory
B territery
C teritory
D territary

EXAMPLE
(A) (B) (C) (D)

ANSWERS
1 (A) (B) (C) (D)
2 (A) (B) (C) (D)
3 (A) (B) (C) (D)
4 (A) (B) (C) (D)
5 (A) (B) (C) (D)
6 (A) (B) (C) (D)
7 (A) (B) (C) (D)
8 (A) (B) (C) (D)
9 (A) (B) (C) (D)
10 (A) (B) (C) (D)

Unit 3 Review (continued)
Activities

What's in a Word?

◆ *century* and *centimeter*
The words *century* and *centimeter* both have a meaning of "one hundred." They come from *centum*, which is the Latin word for 100. Other "100" words that are formed from *centum* include *cent* (1/100 of a dollar), *centennial* (the celebration of a 100th anniversary), and *centipede* (an insect once thought to have 100 legs).

◆ *congratulate*
The word congratulate comes from the same root as the word *grace.* Both words come from the Latin root *gratus,* which means "pleasing." Other words that come from the same root include *congratulations, graceful, graceless,* and *gracious.*

◆ *dictionary*
The word *dictionary* comes from a Latin word meaning "to say" or "to speak." Thus, the literal meaning of the word can be given as "a book of sayings." The idea is that a dictionary records the way people use words as they speak (and as they write).

ROUND ROBIN

In a group with two or three others, write a round-robin story about a day in the life of a person who has moved to your state. As the paper is passed around, each person should add a sentence to the story. The sentence must include one Spelling Word that has not been used in the story before. Keep passing the paper around until you have used all the Spelling Words. Here is an example sentence to get you started. (You don't have to use it.)

"The scenery here is spectacular," thought Isaac, as he viewed the snow-covered mountain.

Spelling Charades

Do this activity with a group. Divide the Spelling Words by the number of people in the group so that each person has four Spelling Words. Each person should write on a slip of paper a mnemonic (a way to remember the word) for each of his or her words. Then all mnemonics should be mixed together. One at a time, each person draws a mnemonic to "act out." Whoever guesses the Spelling Word and correctly spells it is the next to "act out" a mnemonic. Play continues until all mnemonics have been acted out and all words have been spelled correctly.

Your Own Memorial

Do this activity with a partner. Each of you should think about what it would be like to design and construct a memorial to yourself or to a friend. Describe the memorial you would like to create, and explain why it would be appropriate. Then tell how you would go about creating it. Use as many Spelling Words as you can in your description. Exchange papers with your partner, and circle the Spelling Words in each other's papers.

◆ This indicates a Unit Spelling Word.

Unit 3 Review (continued)
Activities

Partner Paragraph

With a partner, take turns writing sentences in a paragraph about a recent project you did at school. Use a Spelling Word in each sentence of your paragraph.

Proofreading Partners

Do this activity with a partner. Each of you should make a list of five Spelling Words that give you trouble or that you think are the most difficult to spell correctly. Exchange lists. Each partner should write a paragraph in which the other person's five words are misspelled. Then exchange papers, and proofread and correct each other's paragraphs. Be sure each Spelling Word is spelled correctly.

Pick a Card, Any Card

Work with a small group, and write each of the Spelling Words on a separate index card. Then place the cards face down on a table, mix them up, and take turns picking one. The person who picks the card says the word, spells it, and then uses it in a sentence.

A Final Scramble

Choose three Spelling Words and scramble the letters in each. Challenge a partner to unscramble the letters and spell each word correctly.

◆ **hurricane**

The word *hurricane* comes from an American Indian word for this kind of storm. The Europeans did not have a word for *hurricane* because true hurricanes do not occur in Europe. The word passed from an American Indian language to Spanish and then eventually to English. The modern spelling of the word in English was influenced by the word *hurry*, because of the idea that a hurricane *hurries* along.

◆ **specialist**

The word *specialist* comes from a Latin word, *specialis*, that means "individual" or "particular." A specialist is someone who has a specialty, or who focuses on one particular thing. A doctor who takes care of children only is a specialist in pediatrics. A teacher who teaches only one subject might be a specialist in that subject. A musician who plays only one kind of music might be a specialist in jazz.

◆ This indicates a Unit Spelling Word.

Lesson 20: More Latin Roots

Spelling Words

1. advise
2. instructions
3. visitors
4. succeeded
5. depositing
6. recess
7. televised
8. revised
9. position
10. constructing
11. composition
12. opposite
13. structures
14. destruction
15. vision
16. necessary

Your Own Words

Look for other words with these Latin roots. You might see *structural* and *concession* in a newspaper article. You might use *postpone* and *visa* when writing a travel essay.

17. _____
18. _____
19. _____
20. _____

Each Spelling Word has a Latin root. Study the words, and look for the Latin root in each word.

Sort the Spelling Words into four groups, according to their Latin roots.

-STRUCT-
_____
_____
_____
_____

-VIS-
_____
_____
_____
_____

-POS(I)T-
_____
_____
_____
_____

-CESS- OR -CEED-
_____
_____
_____
_____

Some English words have Latin roots.

➤ The Latin root *-struct-* means "to build."

➤ The Latin root *-vis-* means "to see."

➤ The Latin root *-pos(i)t-* means "to place or put."

➤ The Latin root *-cess- / -ceed-* means "to yield."

Lesson 20: More Latin Roots (continued)

SPELLING CLUES: Checking Syllables When you proofread your own writing, consider all the syllables in any word you are not certain how to spell. Listen to the sound of each syllable. Make sure you have included all necessary letters to create that sound. Also make sure you have not included any extra letters or syllables.

Look at the two possible spellings. Write the correct spelling of each Spelling Word.

1. oppsite opposite
2. vision vission
3. compostion composition
4. reccess recess
5. depositing depoiteing
6. advize advise

PROOFREADING 7–11. Proofread this newspaper article. Circle the misspelled words. Then write the words correctly on the lines.

ZOO CONSTRUCTION SET TO START

The Civic Zoo Association announced today that two new strucatures will be added to the zoo, providing housing for endangered birds and reptiles. Rainstorms and floods resulted in the detruction of parts of the zoo eighteen months ago. Since then, the Association has succeded in raising funds for a major rebuilding effort. Plans for the enclosures have been reviewed and revized, and workers will begin construcking the addition early next month.

FUN WITH WORDS Write the Spelling Words to replace 12–16.

ATV WELCOMES ALL 12.
BE PART OF THE LIVE
AUDIENCE FOR THE 13
SHOW, *OUR WILD FRIENDS.*

NOTE: EVERY AUDIENCE
MEMBER WILL BE ASSIGNED A
SAFE 14 FOR VIEWING THE
PERFORMANCE.

OK, EDGAR, LET'S GO OVER
YOUR 15 ONE MORE TIME.

ALL RIGHT. BUT TELL ME,
IS ALL THIS MAKEUP
REALLY 16 ?

1. _____
2. _____
3. _____
4. _____
5. _____
6. _____

7. _____
8. _____
9. _____
10. _____
11. _____

12. _____
13. _____
14. _____
15. _____
16. _____

Lesson 21: Unstressed Endings

Spelling Words

1. attendance
2. constant
3. brilliant
4. substance
5. existence
6. incident
7. frequent
8. endurance
9. balance
10. intelligent
11. influence
12. reluctant
13. magnificent
14. experience
15. confidence
16. elegant

Your Own Words

Look for other words with unstressed endings to add to the lists. You might read *incident* and *confidence* in a business letter. You might write *tolerance* and *defiant* in a short story of your own.

17. _____
18. _____
19. _____
20. _____

Each Spelling Word ends with an unstressed syllable. Study the words in the list, and notice how the final syllable of each word is spelled.

Sort the Spelling Words into four groups, according to their endings. Categories have been given for three groups. Fill in the category head for the fourth group as you are sorting.

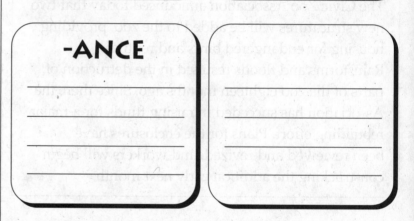

-ANT

_____
_____
_____
_____

-ENT

_____
_____
_____
_____

-ANCE

_____
_____
_____

_____

_____
_____
_____

Some words have similar unstressed endings. These endings may be spelled -*ant* or -*ent*; -*ance* or -*ence*.

Lesson 21: Unstressed Endings *(continued)*

SPELLING CLUES: Comparing Possible Spellings When you are unsure of a word's spelling, write down your best spelling guesses. Compare the possible spellings, and see whether one looks right to you. If you are still not sure, use a dictionary or a glossary to find the correct spelling.

Look at the two possible spellings. Write the correct spelling of each Spelling Word.

1. attendance   attendence
2. elegant   elegent
3. brillient   brilliant

4. substance   substence
5. existence   existance
6. incidant   incident

PROOFREADING 7–12. Proofread the letter below. Circle the misspelled words. Then write the words correctly on the lines.

Hi, Theo!

What a terrific trip we're having! We make frequant stops, and we've been lucky to meet some fascinating people. Yesterday we chatted with a dogsled racer who told us some amazing things about the sport. The dogs—and the sledder—must have incredible endurence. This racer works very hard to balence the dogs on each team. The dogs have to be very intellegent and motivated, since a single dog with a "bad attitude" can infulence the entire team. The man was reluctent to discuss his own races, but we heard later that he is a local champion.

See you in a few more weeks,
Brad

FUN WITH WORDS Write Spelling Words to replace 13–16.

DURING A DOGSLED RACE, DO YOU ADMIRE THE _13_ SCENERY? DO YOU EVER _14_ BOREDOM? DO YOU TALK TO YOURSELF TO BOOST YOUR _15_?

ACTUALLY, MY _16_ WISH IS TO SLEEP IN MY OWN BED AGAIN.

1. _____
2. _____
3. _____
4. _____
5. _____
6. _____

7. _____
8. _____
9. _____
10. _____
11. _____
12. _____

13. _____
14. _____
15. _____
16. _____

Lesson 22: More Latin Roots

Spelling Words

1. permit
2. transfer
3. dismissed
4. suffer
5. transmission
6. contracted
7. commitment
8. attract
9. submit
10. references
11. offered
12. omit
13. admit
14. distract
15. subtraction
16. refer

Your Own Words

Look for other words with these Latin roots to add to the lists. You might read *conference* and *remit* in a news story. You might write *tractor* and *traction* in a story set on a farm.

17. _____
18. _____
19. _____
20. _____

Each Spelling Word has a Latin root. Study the words. Look for the Latin root in each word.

Sort the Spelling Words into three groups, according to their Latin roots. Categories have been given for two groups. Fill in the category head for the third group as you are sorting.

-TRACT-

_____   _____
_____   _____

-MIT- / -MISS-

_____   _____
_____   _____
_____   _____

_____   _____
_____   _____
_____

Some English words have Latin roots.

➤ The Latin root -*tract*- means "to pull or drag."

➤ The Latin root -*mit*-/-*miss*- means "to send."

➤ The Latin root -*fer*- means "to bear or carry."

Lesson 22: More Latin Roots (continued)

SPELLING CLUES: Checking Spelling When you proofread your own writing, read once just for spelling errors. During this reading, ignore the sense of your sentences. Carefully study each word you have written.

Look at these Spelling Words. If the word is misspelled, write it correctly. If the word is not misspelled, place a check mark beside the word and then copy the word.

1. permet   3. dismessed   5. transmision

2. transfir   4. suffer   6. contracked

1. _____

2. _____

3. _____

4. _____

5. _____

6. _____

PROOFREADING 7–12. Proofread these paragraphs. Circle the misspelled words. Then write the words correctly on the lines.

> It takes patience and comitment to gather information about your own genealogy. You can atract the interest— and assistance—of others by talking about your project. Relatives may volunteer to submiss copies of old records for use in your project. A friend's referances to his or her own family tree may lead you to new information about your own. Even strangers can help! A new acquaintance once ofered to look up information about my family during a trip she was taking to explore her own roots.
>
> You should carefully record all the information you gather; it's a mistake to omisse facts from your notes because you're not sure whether or how they are relevant.

7. _____

8. _____

9. _____

10. _____

11. _____

12. _____

FUN WITH WORDS Write Spelling Words to replace 13–16.

JUST 13 THAT YOU HAVE TOO MUCH LUGGAGE.

NOTHING SEEMS TO 14 DEE FROM TAKING PHOTOGRAPHS.

BOB TRIES TO USE 15 INSTEAD OF ADDITION TO FIGURE OUT THE HOTEL BILL.

SHE WANTS TO 16 SUE TO ANOTHER AIRLINE.

13. _____

14. _____

15. _____

16. _____

Lesson 23: Words from French

Spelling Words

1. voyage
2. coupon
3. league
4. prairie
5. portrait
6. buffet
7. ballet
8. bouquet
9. dialogue
10. antique
11. unique
12. vague
13. fatigue
14. technique
15. plaque
16. camouflage

Your Own Words

Look for other words from French to add to the lists. You might notice *courage* in a world history textbook. You might use *crochet* in a description of a craft.

17. _____
18. _____
19. _____
20. _____

Each Spelling Word is derived from a French word. Study the words, and think about the letters that stand for each sound in these words.

Sort the Spelling Words into four groups, according to their endings.

-ET-

_____
_____

-QUE / -GUE

_____ _____

_____ _____

_____ _____

-AGE

_____ _____

OTHER ENDINGS

_____ _____

_____

Some English words are derived from French words. These words may have unusual spellings.

➤ Many words from French end with *-que, -gue, -et,* or *-age.*

Lesson 23: Words from French (continued)

SPELLING CLUES: Visualizing Words When you are learning to spell a difficult word, study it carefully. Think about the pattern of the letters. Then try to visualize that pattern.

Look at the two possible spellings for each Spelling Word. Write the correct spelling.

1. dialogue   dialouge
2. couppon   coupon
3. voage   voyage

4. prairie   praire
5. buffit   buffet

PROOFREADING 6–12. Proofread this journal entry. Circle the misspelled words. Then write the words correctly on the lines.

> I've had vauge feelings of unhappiness all week, and, probably as a result, I'm suffering from fatique today. I think this comes from trying to camouflge my true self. Starting now, I'm going to be me. I am confident that I don't have to look exactly like every other member of the soccer leage. I know that in art class I don't have to use exactly the same technic as everyone else or, for that matter, paint the same kind of portrette. Starting now, I'm ready to think of myself not as weird, but as unikue.

FUN WITH WORDS Write Spelling Words to replace 13–16.

1. _____
2. _____
3. _____
4. _____
5. _____

6. _____
7. _____
8. _____
9. _____
10. _____
11. _____
12. _____
13. _____
14. _____
15. _____
16. _____

Watch our dancers leap and sway. Take a seat for the __13__.

It's no longer new and sleek. It's nice and old—a fine __14__.

Send some lovely flowers on their way. Let us deliver your special __15__.

How many blocks can you add to this stack? If you top 100, you'll win a __16__.

Lesson 24: Related Words

Spelling Words

1. history
2. historical
3. family
4. familiar
5. fantasy
6. fantastic
7. company
8. companion
9. editor
10. editorial
11. colony
12. colonial
13. strategy
14. strategic
15. diplomacy
16. diplomatic

Your Own Words

Look for other pairs of related words to add to the lists. You might see *Italy* and *Italian* in a travel brochure. You might use *mystery* and *mysterious* when you write your own scary short story.

17. _____
18. _____
19. _____
20. _____

Each Spelling Word is one of a pair of related words. Look at the words in pairs, and think about how the second word in each pair is related to the first. Notice that the first word in each pair has the sound in its next-to-last syllable. That sound changes—although the vowel spelling does not change—when a suffix is added to form the second word in the pair.

Sort the pairs of Spelling Words into three groups, according to the changes in vowel sounds.

TO R-CONTROLLED VOWEL

_____ _____

_____ _____

TO SHORT VOWEL

_____ _____

_____ _____

_____ _____

_____ _____

TO LONG VOWEL

_____ _____

_____ _____

Many words are formed by the addition of a suffix to a base word. The addition of a suffix may change the vowel sound—but not the vowel spelling—near the end of the base word.

Lesson 24: Related Words (continued)

SPELLING CLUES: Checking Base Words When you write a word with a suffix, think about the spelling of the base word. Make sure you spell the base word correctly. Then make spelling changes required by the addition of the suffix.

Look at the two possible spellings for each Spelling Word. Write the correct spelling.

1. stratiegic   strategic
2. diplomacy   diplomecy
3. editer   editor

4. histry   history
5. company   compeny
6. historial   historical

1. _____
2. _____
3. _____
4. _____
5. _____
6. _____

PROOFREADING 7–12. Proofread this letter. Circle the misspelled words. Then write the words correctly on the lines.

Dear Gram,
    I'm having a great time—and learning a lot! We went diving yesterday and saw a huge coloney of sponges growing on the bottom of the bay. We also saw some colorful coral. I learned that, like the sponge, coral is a coloanial animal. (Don't tell the rest of the famly, but until then I had thought coral was a rock!) The underwater colors are fantasic—bright blues and yellows and even pinks! I know you're familar with all these sights, because you've been diving here yourself.
    This trip is like a fanasy come true for me— I can't wait to come back!

                                        Love,
                                        Rosa

7. _____
8. _____
9. _____
10. _____
11. _____
12. _____

FUN WITH WORDS Write Spelling Words for 13–16.

13. If you want to win a game of chess, you need this.
14. If you want to get along well with other people, you need to be this.
15. If you want to express you own opinion—not just the facts—in a newspaper, you need to write this.
16. If you want to take a trip, but you're not allowed to go alone, you need this.

13. _____
14. _____
15. _____
16. _____

Lesson 25: More Related Words

Spelling Words

1. resignation
2. receipt
3. heir
4. softened
5. hasten
6. autumn
7. autumnal
8. softly
9. heritage
10. designated
11. designed
12. reception
13. signature
14. haste
15. sign
16. resign

Your Own Words

Look for other pairs of related words to add to the lists. You might read *deceive* and *deception* in a mystery story. You might write *reject* and *rejection* in a letter of complaint.

17. _____
18. _____
19. _____
20. _____

Each Spelling Word represents part of a word family. Look at the words in pairs, and think about how the two words in each pair are related.

Sort the pairs of Spelling Words into two groups. In the first group, write the pairs in which the addition of the suffix does not change the spelling of the base word. In the second group, write the pairs in which the spelling of the base word changes with the addition of the suffix.

NO SPELLING CHANGE

_____ _____
_____ _____
_____ _____
_____ _____
_____ _____

SPELLING CHANGE

_____ _____
_____ _____

Many words are formed by the addition of a suffix to a base word. In some words, the addition of the suffix does not change the spelling of the base word.

Lesson 25: More Related Words (continued)

SPELLING CLUES: Checking Spelling When you proofread your own writing, read once just for spelling errors. During this reading, ignore the sense of your sentences. Carefully study each word you have written.

Proofread these Spelling Words. If the word is misspelled, write it correctly. If the word is not misspelled, place a check mark beside the word and then copy the word.

1. hast
2. autumal
3. hier
4. softened
5. heiritage

1. _____
2. _____
3. _____
4. _____
5. _____

PROOFREADING 6–12. Proofread the newspaper editorial. Circle the misspelled words. Then write the words correctly on the lines.

CALL FOR BODINE TO STEP DOWN

The *City News* joins local leaders in calling for the resingation of Joseph Bodine as head of our Animal Protection League. The first sign of trouble surfaced last autum, with reports that puppies were being given to children without the consent of their parents. At that time, the *City News* reprinted a reciept for a ten-week-old puppy. It had the signiture of an eight-year-old.

Since then, two City Council members have been desinnated to investigate League practices. However, Bodine has refused to cooperate. In light of this, the *City News* urges Mayor Chu to ask Bodine to resine. If he refuses, we feel strongly that the Mayor must hassen to fire Bodine.

6. _____
7. _____
8. _____
9. _____
10. _____
11. _____
12. _____
13. _____
14. _____
15. _____
16. _____

FUN WITH WORDS Write Spelling Words to replace 13–16.

Unit 4 Review
Practice Test: Part A

Read the possible spellings for each word. Mark the letter
of the correctly spelled word.

EXAMPLE:

A birth day   C berthday
B birth-day   D birthday

1. A portrait   C portrat
   B portait   D pertrait

2. A familar   C familyar
   B familiar   D familer

3. A suceded   C succeded
   B suceeded   D succeeded

4. A confidense   C confidence
   B confedence   D confidince

5. A dialoq   C dialogue
   B dialoque   D dialgue

6. A magnificent   C magnificant
   B magnifacent   D magnifisent

7. A transmision   C tranzmission
   B transmisson   D transmission

8. A permitt   C permit
   B perrmit   D perrmitt

9. A committment   C comitment
   B comittment   D commitment

10. A receipt   C reciept
    B recept   D receit

EXAMPLE

(A) (B) (C) ●D

ANSWERS

1 (A) (B) (C) (D)

2 (A) (B) (C) (D)

3 (A) (B) (C) (D)

4 (A) (B) (C) (D)

5 (A) (B) (C) (D)

6 (A) (B) (C) (D)

7 (A) (B) (C) (D)

8 (A) (B) (C) (D)

9 (A) (B) (C) (D)

10 (A) (B) (C) (D)

Unit 4 Review *(continued)*
Practice Test: Part B

Fill in the letter of the correctly spelled word.

EXAMPLE: Do you have <u>change</u> for a <u>qarter</u>?
    A   B

1. Dancing <u>ballet</u> tends to <u>fatige</u> me.
    A   B

2. She was <u>ofered</u> the position because her <u>references</u>
    A   B
were excellent.

3. This <u>cupon</u> gets you a free <u>voyage</u>.
    A   B

4. His most recent job <u>experience</u> gave him the
    A
<u>confidance</u> to apply for another position.
    B

5. The visitors followed <u>enstructions</u>.
    <u>A</u>   B

6. Did you study <u>coloneal</u> <u>history</u>?
    A   B

7. The <u>autum</u> leaves fall <u>softly</u>.
    A   B

8. He put his <u>signature</u> on the <u>rezignation</u>.
    A   B

9. Her <u>strategy</u> will <u>hassen</u> matters.
    A   B

10. We designed the <u>plack</u> of honor.
    A   B

EXAMPLE

Ⓐ   Ⓑ

ANSWERS

1   Ⓐ   Ⓑ

2   Ⓐ   Ⓑ

3   Ⓐ   Ⓑ

4   Ⓐ   Ⓑ

5   Ⓐ   Ⓑ

6   Ⓐ   Ⓑ

7   Ⓐ   Ⓑ

8   Ⓐ   Ⓑ

9   Ⓐ   Ⓑ

10   Ⓐ   Ⓑ

Unit 4 Review *(continued)*
Activities

What's in a Word?

affection
Affection comes from the Latin word *affectio*, from the verb *afficere*, meaning "to influence." Today the word usually means "a feeling of fondness or love."

◆ autumn
The word *autumn* comes from *autumnus*, the Latin name for this season. *Autumn's* more common synonym, which is *fall*, comes from an Old English word and is probably related to words from Old German, Old Norse, and Lithuanian.

◆ commitment
Commitment is a noun formed by adding the suffix *-ment* to the verb *commit*. Commit can be traced to an ancient Latin word that includes the prefix *com-*, meaning "with," and the verb *mittere*, meaning "to send or give over." The prefix *com-*, sometimes also spelled *con-*, is part of many familiar English words. Commitment is a feature of the main characters in many books.

endurance
The root of the word *endurance* comes from the ancient Latin verb *durare*, meaning "to harden." You can identify the same root in the English words *durable*, *duress*, *duration*, and *during*. Characters in many stories show determination and endurance.

Synonym/Antonym Spelling

Work with a partner to review at least five Spelling Words. Give your partner either a synonym or an antonym of a Spelling Word as a clue. Be sure to tell which you are using—a synonym or an antonym. Then ask your partner to guess and spell the word.

ENDURANCE SPELLING

With a partner, play a game to review the Spelling Words. Read the words, and ask your partner to spell each word aloud as quickly as possible. Then switch roles. Which of you can *endure* the pressure and spell all the words correctly?

Picture Clues

Do this activity with a partner. Each partner should draw simple characters or scenes as clues to three different Spelling Words. Trade drawings with your partner. Identify and write the correct Spelling Word under each of your partner's clues.

Spelling Crossword

Review the Spelling Words, and choose at least seven words to use in a crossword puzzle. Plan where each word will go in your puzzle, remembering that each word should share a letter with at least one other word. Draw a box for every letter of each word. Use other words to fill out your puzzle. Then write clues for each word. Ask a classmate to solve your puzzle.

◆ This indicates a Unit Spelling Word.

Unit 4 Review (continued)
Activities

YOUR OWN USAGE NOTES

With a partner, select four Spelling Words. Write usage notes—explanations or reminders for using words—for each of those words, with a reminder or an explanation of the correct current usage. (You may want to refer to a dictionary or another reference work.) Share your usage notes with the rest of the class.

Proofreading Partners

Do this activity with a partner. Each of you should make a list of five Spelling Words that give you trouble or that you consider challenging to spell correctly. Exchange lists. Each partner should write a paragraph on any topic you choose. Use your partner's five Spelling Words in your paragraph, but misspell them. Then exchange papers, and proofread and correct each other's paragraphs. Be sure each Spelling Word is spelled correctly.

Suspenseful Titles

Stories that are suspenseful often have titles that suggest a mystery or some danger. Work in a small group, and make up titles for suspenseful stories. Use some of the Spelling Words.

Partner Spelling

Write clues for five Spelling Words. Then switch clues with a partner. Write the Spelling Words that match your partner's clues. Then change papers again and check each other's answers.

What's in a Word?

◆ **family**
The word *family* comes from the Latin word *familia*, meaning "household." In ancient Rome, the *familia* included everyone who lived within the house—relatives and servants. Over time, patterns of living change, and so do the meanings of words. Families and family relationships are important in many stories.

◆ **portrait**
The word *portrait* has an interesting history. We now use the word to mean "a drawing, painting, or photograph of a person, showing especially the face" or "a vivid or imaginative description." The word comes to us from a French word, which in turn derives from the Latin verb *protrahere*, meaning "to reveal." A portrait often reveals a great deal about a person's personality and emotions, as well as depicting his or her appearance.

◆ **unique**
Unique is a very strong word that means "one of a kind." It's better not to weaken this word by saying that something is "rather unique" or "very unique."

◆ This indicates a Unit Spelling Word.

Lesson 27: Greek Word Parts

Spelling Words

1. geography
2. photograph
3. paragraph
4. thermometer
5. diameter
6. graph
7. meters
8. astronomer
9. barometer
10. biography
11. astronaut
12. kilometers
13. astronomy
14. photography
15. centimeters
16. autograph

Your Own Words

Look for other words with these Greek word parts. You might find *disaster* or *telegraph* in a first-person account of an early twentieth-century shipwreck.

17. _____
18. _____
19. _____
20. _____

Each Spelling Word has a Greek word part. Study the word, and find the Greek word part in each word.

Sort the Spelling Words into three groups according to their Greek word parts. Category heads have been given for two groups. Fill in the category head for the third group as you are sorting.

-AST(E)R-
asterisk

_____   _____

_____

-GRAPH-
telegraph

_____   _____

_____   _____

_____

_____   _____

_____

Some English words have Greek word parts. Knowing the meaning of Greek word parts can help you understand many English words.

➤ The word part *-ast(e)r-* means "star."

➤ The word part *-graph-* means "write."

➤ The word part *-meter-* means "measure."

Lesson 27: Greek Word Parts (continued)

SPELLING CLUES: Greek Word Parts When you write a word that includes a Greek word part, make sure you spell the word part correctly. Then decide if the rest of the word is also spelled accurately.

Read the phrases below. Determine what missing word part is needed to spell each Spelling Word correctly. Then write the Spelling Words to replace 1–5.

an infrared photo __1__

a Greek __2__onomer

three centi__3__ in diameter

geo__4__y of the planet Earth

write a para__5__

PROOFREADING 6–10. Correct this transmission to a rescue vehicle on Mercury by circling each misspelled word. Write the words correctly on the lines.

> SOS. STATION THERMOMITER READS 49 DEGREES
> CELSIUS. HEAT DEFLECTORS INADEQUATE. READINGS
> ON BAROMITRE PREDICT ANOTHER SOLAR STORM
> BEFORE NIGHTFALL. RADAR REPORTS YOUR LOCATION
> AS 1,735 KILAMETERS EAST. TRAVELING AT 321 KPH.
> PLEASE CONFIRM ASAP. STATION CANNOT RIDE OUT
> ANOTHER STORM. IN EVENT OF OUR DEMISE, CAPTAIN'S
> LOG AND BIOGAPHY BURIED 15 METRES DUE EAST OF
> HQ AT LOCATOR SHAFT.

WORKING WITH MEANING Write the Spelling Word that goes with each phrase or sentence below.

11. diagram comparing one or more things
12. capturing images

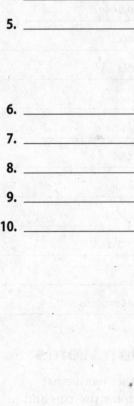

13. Galileo would have earned an A+ in this subject
14. a pair of radii
15. a name you can sell
16. a space pioneer

1. _____
2. _____
3. _____
4. _____
5. _____

6. _____
7. _____
8. _____
9. _____
10. _____

11. _____
12. _____
13. _____
14. _____
15. _____
16. _____

Lesson 28: Number Prefixes

Spelling Words

1. December
2. October
3. quart
4. bicycle
5. trio
6. monopoly
7. quartet
8. tricycle
9. decade
10. octopus
11. decimal
12. quarters
13. triangles
14. binoculars
15. triple
16. monotonous

Your Own Words

Look for other words that include number prefixes and combining forms. You might find *decathlon* or *quarterback* in a book about sports. You might find *quadrangle* or *binary* in a math book.

17. _____
18. _____
19. _____
20. _____

Each Spelling Word begins with a number prefix or combining form. Study the words.

Sort the Spelling Words into groups.

DEC- / DECI-
decimeter

_____
_____
_____

OCT-
octane

_____
_____

QUADR- (QUART-)
quadruple

_____
_____
_____

BI-
biannual

_____
_____

MON- / MONO-
monarch

_____
_____

TRI-
triathlon

_____
_____
_____

mon-/mono- = "one"   bi- = "two"   tri- = "three"
quad- = "four"   oct- = "eight"   dec-/deci- = "ten"

Lesson 28: Number Prefixes *(continued)*

SPELLING CLUES: Checking Number Prefixes and Combining Forms Knowing common number prefixes and combining forms can help you understand and spell many English words.

Look at the two possible spellings for each Spelling Word. Write the correct spelling.

1. October   Octber   4. triple   tripel
2. treo   trio   5. menotonous   monotonous
3. desimal   decimal   6. traingles   triangles

PROOFREADING 7–12. Elena has made a list of things to take on a cross-country bike tour. Here is a portion of the list. Circle the misspelled words. Then write the words correctly on the lines.

> bycicle
> daypack
> quat bottle for water
> instant lemonade
> pocket journal for Decmber
> beefsticks
> dried fruit
> directions to sleeping quaters
> maps
> pocket Monoply game
> sunblock
> benoculars

FUN WITH WORDS Write a Spelling Word for each silly definition below. Of course, these aren't real definitions of the words.

13. a cat with eight sides
14. singing fours
15. a bike for triplets
16. a thirst-quencher for ten-year-olds

1. _____
2. _____
3. _____
4. _____
5. _____
6. _____

7. _____
8. _____
9. _____
10. _____
11. _____
12. _____

13. _____
14. _____
15. _____
16. _____

Lesson 29: Spelling and Pronunciation

Spelling Words

1. drowned
2. restaurant
3. ivory
4. chocolate
5. desperate
6. lightning
7. adjective
8. penetrate
9. aspirin
10. athletes
11. identity
12. disastrous
13. ecstatic
14. platinum
15. incidentally
16. tentatively

Your Own Words

Look for other words commonly misspelled because they are sometimes mispronounced to add to the lists. You might find *dangerous* or *thorough* in a detective story.

17. _____
18. _____
19. _____
20. _____

Earlier in this book, you studied words that are commonly misspelled because they are commonly mispronounced. Here are some more. Look at each Spelling Word.

Sort the words according to the categories listed below.

OMITTED SYLLABLE
interest

_____
_____
_____
_____
_____
_____

OMITTED LETTER
breadth

_____
_____
_____
_____
_____
_____

ADDED SYLLABLE
athletics

_____   _____
_____   _____
_____

Frequently mispronounced words are also often misspelled. To spell a word correctly, think about the correct pronunciation.

Lesson 29: Spelling and Pronunciation *(continued)*

SPELLING CLUES: Commonly Misspelled Words Some words are difficult to spell because they are often mispronounced. Sometimes saying a word aloud or silently to yourself will help you know how to spell it correctly.

Read each word below. Decide if a letter or letters are missing or if there are extra letters. Then write the correct spelling of each Spelling Word.

1. choclate
2. ajective
3. platnum
4. eckstatic
5. incidently
6. lightening
7. drownd
8. disasterous

1. _____
2. _____
3. _____
4. _____
5. _____
6. _____
7. _____
8. _____

PROOFREADING 9–12. Circle the misspelled words below. Then write the words correctly on the lines.

> Patient came in with severe lacerations to the right thumb.
>
> Identy of bird causing lacerations unknown; however, claw was allowed to pentrate 3–4 millimeters before patient was able to free himself.
>
> I removed a 1-millimeter piece of claw (ivery in color) from patient's thumb, treated the wound, and applied a bandage.
>
> Patient told to take asprin for pain and released from care.

9. _____
10. _____
11. _____
12. _____

FUN WITH WORDS Circle the misspelled words in the cartoon below. Write each Spelling Word correctly.

THAT NEW RESTURANT IS OWNED BY THREE FAMOUS ATHELETES.

I'M DESPRATE TO GO. CAN YOU HAVE LUNCH ON SATURDAY?

TENTIVELY YES. I HAVE TO ASK MY PARENTS.

13. _____
14. _____
15. _____
16. _____

Lesson 30: Clipped Words

Spelling Words

1. automobile
2. necktie
3. refrigerator
4. gasoline
5. caravan
6. luncheon
7. champion
8. gymnasium
9. laboratory
10. mathematics
11. parachute
12. submarine
13. teenagers
14. memorandum
15. limousine
16. examination

Your Own Words

Look for other words that are sometimes clipped to add to the lists. You might see *veterinarian* in a book about animals. You might use *telephone* when writing about twentieth-century inventions.

17. _____
18. _____
19. _____
20. _____

Each Spelling Word is often shortened, or clipped, to form another word. Usually words that get clipped are long and used frequently, but even fairly short words may get clipped.

Sort the Spelling Words in a way that will help you remember them. Example words have been given.

taxicab
_____
_____
_____
_____
_____
_____
_____
_____
_____
_____

hamburger
_____
_____
_____

embankment
_____
_____

Clipped words are shortened forms of longer words.

➤ **The shortened form may be the beginning, the middle, or the ending of the longer word.**

➤ **Once you can spell the clipped word, concentrate on correctly spelling the other syllables of the longer word.**

Lesson 30: Clipped Words (continued)

SPELLING CLUES: Clipped Forms The clipped form of a word is often used in informal writing. In formal writing, the longer version of the word may be more appropriate.

Look at each clipped word. Determine the word from which it came. Write the correct Spelling Word.

1. gas
2. van
3. auto
4. sub

5. chute
6. memo
7. exam

1. _____
2. _____
3. _____
4. _____
5. _____
6. _____
7. _____

PROOFREADING 8–11.   Circle each misspelled word. Then write the words correctly on the lines.

Dear Koby,
  Guess what! When I get back, my favorite class won't be in the gymnassium anymore. It'll be in the science labarotory. Surprise! After this summer, I'm looking forward to studying biology. Nature is amazing! Who cares if I'm not a champain basketball player? I'm too short anyway. One problem: Do you think biologists have to be good in mathimattics? Oh well. How's your summer going?

                                        Sincerely,
                                        Lindsey

8. _____
9. _____
10. _____
11. _____

FUN WITH WORDS Replace the underlined clipped words in the cartoons. Write the correct Spelling Word.

12. _____
13. _____
14. _____
15. _____
16. _____

Unit 5 Review
Practice Test: Part A

Read each group of phrases. Find the underlined word that is misspelled. Fill in the answer circle for that phrase.

EXAMPLE:

A tipped the <u>canoe</u>   C hurried <u>home</u>
B twisted an <u>ankel</u>   D <u>concentrated</u> hard

1. A experienced <u>astronaut</u>   C read the <u>barometer</u>
   B wrote a <u>memorandum</u>   D took a <u>photograf</u>

2. A rode a <u>bicycle</u>   C the first of <u>Decembre</u>
   B a <u>decade</u> ago   D an <u>October</u> holiday

3. A twelve <u>centemeters</u>   C studied <u>astronomy</u>
   B wrote a <u>biography</u>   D taught <u>geography</u>

4. A draw a <u>graph</u>   C <u>decimil</u> point
   B use a <u>thermometer</u>   D <u>quart</u> of milk

5. A noted <u>astronomer</u>   C held a <u>monopoly</u>
   B measured the <u>diameter</u>   D wore a <u>neck</u> tie

6. A <u>monotanous</u> task   C use <u>binoculars</u>
   B <u>triple</u> play   D study <u>photography</u>

7. A nine <u>kilometers</u>   C draw <u>triangels</u>
   B write a <u>paragraph</u>   D ride a <u>tricycle</u>

8. A string <u>quartet</u>   C take <u>aspirin</u>
   B colorful <u>ajective</u>   D <u>chocolate</u> cake

9. A able <u>atheletes</u>   C <u>disastrous</u> results
   B <u>desperate</u> attempt   D <u>drowned</u> in water

10. A attended a <u>luncheon</u>   C mentioned <u>incidently</u>
    B known <u>identity</u>   D thunder and <u>lightning</u>

EXAMPLE

(A) (B) (C) (D)

ANSWERS

1 (A) (B) (C) (D)
2 (A) (B) (C) (D)
3 (A) (B) (C) (D)
4 (A) (B) (C) (D)
5 (A) (B) (C) (D)
6 (A) (B) (C) (D)
7 (A) (B) (C) (D)
8 (A) (B) (C) (D)
9 (A) (B) (C) (D)
10 (A) (B) (C) (D)

Unit 5 Review *(continued)*
Practice Test: Part B

My friends and I took a <u>bycycle</u> trip across the United States. It wasn't as comfortable as

          1

driving in an <u>autamobile</u>; however, the trip was never <u>monnotonous</u>. Our <u>careavan</u>

         2   3   4

managed to <u>penitrate</u> the wide open spaces of America. At each site, one of us took a

         5

<u>photgrah</u> as a keepsake. Our <u>examinashun</u> of the country was fascinating! Each <u>restraunt</u>

 6   7   8

served interesting regional foods. I wish we'd had a portable <u>refrigerater</u> to store

                                       9

them in! Best of all, our souvenirs from the trip included

an <u>autgraph</u> from a famous movie star!

   10

The number of each set matches the number of an underlined word above. Mark the letter of the correctly spelled word.

1. A bicicle   C bycyle
    B bycicle   D bicycle

2. A autamabile   C automobile
    B automabile   D automobil

3. A monotonous   C menotonous
    B monottonous   D monotous

4. A carovan   C carvan
    B caravon   D caravan

5. A penetrate   C penitrait
    B penetrait   D penetrayt

6. A fotograph   C photograh
    B photograph   D photgraph

7. A examination   C ixamination
    B examanation   D examanashun

8. A restrunt   C restaurant
    B resterant   D restrant

9. A refrigrator   C refrigerator
    B refrigrater   D refrigeratur

10. A autograh   C auttograph
     B autigraph   D autograph

ANSWERS

1 Ⓐ Ⓑ Ⓒ Ⓓ

2 Ⓐ Ⓑ Ⓒ Ⓓ

3 Ⓐ Ⓑ Ⓒ Ⓓ

4 Ⓐ Ⓑ Ⓒ Ⓓ

5 Ⓐ Ⓑ Ⓒ Ⓓ

6 Ⓐ Ⓑ Ⓒ Ⓓ

7 Ⓐ Ⓑ Ⓒ Ⓓ

8 Ⓐ Ⓑ Ⓒ Ⓓ

9 Ⓐ Ⓑ Ⓒ Ⓓ

10 Ⓐ Ⓑ Ⓒ Ⓓ

Unit 5 Review (continued)
Activities

What's in a Word?

◆ *astronaut*
Astronaut is a modern word that was formed by combining two ancient Greek words. *Astronaut* literally means "star traveler."

camera
Our word *camera* comes from *camera obscura* (meaning "dark room" in Latin). The first accounts of a *camera obscura* come from the tenth century. By the early sixteenth century, the *camera obscura* was used to project images on walls so that they could be clearly drawn. Today, photography, once an aid in sketching, has often replaced realistic drawing. For example, naturalists once sketched the wildlife they observed, but now they usually take photographs.

◆ *chocolate*
Our word *chocolate* comes from Mexico. Chocolate was a favorite drink of the Aztecs centuries ago. Spanish explorers brought chocolate to Europe about A.D. 1500. It didn't take long for chocolate to become popular. Chocolate was first manufactured in the American colonies in 1765. Although it was the Swiss who perfected the processing of milk chocolate in about 1876, the United States remains the world's leading chocolate producer.

◆ This indicates a Unit Spelling Word.

Secret Messages

Do this activity with a partner. Each of you should write a secret message using abbreviations. Exchange secret messages, and figure out what word each abbreviation stands for. Write the words. Then exchange papers again, and check that the correct word has been used in place of each abbreviation.

Say It Quickly

Play this game in a group. The goal is speed. Going clockwise, players take turns naming number prefixes or combining forms, such as *demi-*, *pent-*, *hex-*, *hept-*, *cent-*, *kilo-*. As soon as a player names a prefix or a combining form, anyone can call out a word that begins with the prefix or combining form. The first person to say a word beginning with that prefix or combining form gets a point, and the person who called out the prefix or combining form writes the word down. Then the next person in the circle calls out a prefix or a combining form, and the game continues. The player with the most points wins.

Tongue Twisters

Write a short tongue twister that includes at least three Spelling Words. Have a classmate check your spelling before he or she attempts to say the tongue twister faster.

Unit 5 Review (continued)
Activities

Proofreading Partners

Do this activity with a partner. Each of you should make a list of five Spelling Words that give you trouble or that you need to think about before you spell them correctly. Exchange lists. Each partner should write a paragraph in which the other person's five words are misspelled. Then exchange papers, and proofread and correct each other's paragraphs. Be sure each Spelling Word is spelled correctly.

SPELLING DUET

Do this activity with a partner. Write each Spelling Word on a slip of paper. Fold the slips and put them in a container or a pile. Take turns choosing a word and giving your partner as many one-word clues as necessary until he or she guesses the Spelling Word and spells it correctly. An example of a series of clues would be *glasses*, *birds*, *far* (binoculars).

Hiking Partners

Do this activity with a partner. Each of you should write a paragraph about some kind of hiking adventure. Use five Spelling Words in your paragraph, but don't write down the Spelling Words. Instead, leave blanks where the Spelling Words should go. Exchange papers, and fill in the five Spelling Words that are missing from your partner's paragraph. Then exchange papers again, and check each other's spelling.

What's in a Word?

hearth
The word *hearth* conjures up feelings of warmth, security, and family. From earliest times, humankind has gathered around a hearth—whether in a cave or in a modern house.

◆ *restaurant*
The word *restaurant* is related to the word *restore*. The idea is that eating food in a restaurant can *restore* your strength or health. Because eating is such an essential part of life, you might think that *restaurant* is an ancient word. Surprisingly, however, restaurants have existed only since the 1700s.

satellite
The word *satellite* comes from the Latin word *satelles*, meaning "attendant or follower." In fact, *satellite* still can mean this. Today we are more familiar with other meanings. For example, when we think of satellites, we may think of the moon or the Hubble space telescope.

◆ This indicates a Unit Spelling Word.

Lesson 32: More Greek Word Parts

Spelling Words

1. scope
2. carbohydrate
3. microscope
4. catalog
5. logic
6. biology
7. monologue
8. hydrant
9. technology
10. analogy
11. mythology
12. apologizing
13. periscope
14. telescope
15. dehydrated
16. psychology

Your Own Words

Look for other words with these Greek word parts. You might read a book about *astrology* to find out about your *horoscope* in a newspaper. You might use *hydroelectric* or *ecology* in a report on energy.

17. _____
18. _____
19. _____
20. _____

Each Spelling Word includes one of the following Greek word parts: *-hydr-, -ology, -log-,* or *-scop-*. These Greek word parts, along with many others, form the basis of hundreds of words in the English language.

Look at the words and pronounce each one carefully. Think about the meaning of the Greek word part found in the word. Then sort the Spelling Words into groups.

-HYDR-
_____
_____
_____

-LOG-
_____
_____
_____
_____

-OLOGY
_____
_____
_____
_____

-SCOP-
_____
_____
_____
_____

Knowing the meaning of the Greek word parts *-hydr-,* *-log-, -ology,* and *-scop-* may help you spell many words derived from them.

➤ The Greek word part *-hydr-* means "water."

➤ The Greek word part *-ology* means "the study of" or "the science of."

➤ The Greek word part *-log-* means "word."

➤ The Greek word part *-scop-* means "see."

Lesson 32: More Greek Word Parts (continued)

SPELLING CLUES: Word Parts Use your knowledge of word parts when you check your spelling. If you think about the meaning of a word, you can often determine whether the word contains a familiar word part or root. Then make sure the word part or root is spelled as you know it should be.

Proofread these words and decide which of each pair is correct. Circle the word that is correctly spelled. Then write the correct spelling of each Spelling Word.

1. monologue   3. hidrant   5. apologizing
   monalogue   hydrant   apoligizing

2. logick   4. periscope   6. analigy
   logic   perascope   analogy

1. _____
2. _____
3. _____
4. _____
5. _____
6. _____

PROOFREADING 7–12. Read the six rules for runners below. Circle the misspelled word in each rule. Then write the words correctly on the lines.

- Psycology is important—learn to think like a winner!
- Stock up on energy before a race. Food with a high carbohidrate content will keep you going.
- It's easy to become dehydrayted on a long run in hot weather. Drink plenty of water before a race.
- Make sure the skope of any training program you begin includes a variety of exercises.
- Tecnology has given athletes a tremendous variety of sports gear to choose from. Choose comfortable running shoes.
- Most books on running include a catolog of runners' ailments. See a doctor if you have a running-related injury.

7. _____
8. _____
9. _____
10. _____
11. _____
12. _____

WORKING WITH MEANING Write the Spelling Word that answers each question.

13. What would you read to learn about the Greek gods?
14. What instrument would you use to see the planets?
15. What instrument would you use to study tiny plants?
16. What subject would you explore to find out how living things grow?

13. _____
14. _____
15. _____
16. _____

Lesson 33: Words with Many Syllables

Spelling Words

1. cooperation
2. organization
3. administration
4. autobiography
5. agricultural
6. identification
7. encyclopedia
8. possibility
9. exceptionally
10. responsibilities
11. characteristic
12. recommendation
13. rehabilitation
14. acceleration
15. simultaneously
16. accumulation

Your Own Words

Look for other words with five or more syllables. You might find *quadrilateral* in a math word problem. You might use *intergalactic* or *extraterrestrial* in a science fiction story.

17. _____
18. _____
19. _____
20. _____

Each Spelling Word has either five or six syllables. Like these words, many long words in English are made up of Greek or Latin word parts to which prefixes or suffixes have been added.

Look at each word and pronounce each syllable carefully. Look for base words, word parts, and prefixes and suffixes. Then sort the Spelling Words into two groups based on the number of syllables.

WORDS WITH FIVE SYLLABLES

_____
_____
_____
_____
_____
_____
_____
_____

WORDS WITH SIX SYLLABLES

_____
_____
_____
_____
_____
_____

The spelling of most long words follow their pronunciation closely.

➤ **Figure out the spelling of smaller words or base words first, such as *recommend* in *recommendation*.**

➤ **Then spell the prefixes and suffixes.**

Lesson 33: Words with Many Syllables *(continued)*

SPELLING CLUES: Pronunciation When you spell a word that has many syllables, pronounce the word slowly and carefully. Then think about the spelling of each part of the word. Since many spelling difficulties occur in syllables with unstressed vowels, use your knowledge of prefixes, suffixes, and word parts to help with these syllables.

Proofread these words and decide which spelling in each pair is correct. Circle the word that is correctly spelled. Then write the correct spelling of each Spelling Word.

1. autobiogrophy
   autobiography
3. accumulation
   accummulation
5. axceleration
   acceleration

2. coaperation
   cooperation
4. simultanously
   simultaneously
6. agricultural
   agracultural

PROOFREADING 7–12. Proofread the following sentences. Circle the misspelled word in each sentence. Then write the words correctly on the lines.

- Scientists, pet owners, and volunteers help in the adminestration of programs to train working animals.
- International Hearing Dog is an organazation that trains dogs to assist hearing-impaired people.
- Some animals assist in the physical rehabilatation of people who have been injured.
- Working animals wear laminated idenification cards.
- The responsabilities of people with working dogs include managing their dogs' behavior.
- Specialists sometimes make a recomendation concerning an animal's suitability for training.

FUN WITH WORDS Write Spelling Words to replace 13–16.

1. _____
2. _____
3. _____
4. _____
5. _____
6. _____

7. _____
8. _____
9. _____
10. _____
11. _____
12. _____
13. _____
14. _____
15. _____
16. _____

WHAT IS THE __13__ OF MY FRIEND'S ENTERING YOUR TRAINING PROGRAM?

ANY ANIMAL IN OUR PROGRAM NEEDS TO BE __14__ INTELLIGENT.

IF YOU HAVE READ THE __15__, AS I HAVE, YOU WOULD KNOW THAT A MAJOR __16__ OF MONKEYS IS THEIR INTELLIGENCE.

Lesson 34: More Latin Roots

Spelling Words

1. reform _____
2. respiration _____
3. formation _____
4. inspiration _____
5. inspired _____
6. convention _____
7. formula _____
8. adventure _____
9. depends _____
10. uniform _____
11. inventor _____
12. pending _____
13. invention _____
14. transformed _____
15. perform _____
16. suspended _____

Your Own Words

Look for other words with the Latin root -ven-, -spir-, -form-, or -pend-. You might see independent or unconventional in a character sketch. You might use information or appendix in a research paper.

17. _____
18. _____
19. _____
20. _____

Each Spelling Word includes the Latin root -spir-, -form-, -ven-, or -pend-. Like these words, hundreds of words in the English language consist of Latin roots to which prefixes and suffixes have been added.

As you look at each word, think about the meaning of the root. Then sort the Spelling Words into four groups.

-SPIR-
_____
_____
_____

-VEN-
_____
_____
_____
_____

-FORM-
_____
_____
_____
_____
_____

-PEND-
_____
_____
_____

In general, the spelling of words with Latin roots closely follows their pronunciation. The more familiar you become with common roots, prefixes, and suffixes, the more easily you will be able to spell these words.

➤ The Latin root -spir- means "breathe."

➤ The Latin root -form- means "shape."

➤ The Latin root -ven- means "come."

➤ The Latin root -pend- means "hang."

Lesson 34: More Latin Roots (continued)

SPELLING CLUES: Roots, Prefixes, and Suffixes If you have difficulty spelling a word, listen for roots or word parts you recognize. Think about how those are spelled in words more familiar to you. Then identify any prefixes or suffixes in the word, and again use your knowledge of other words as a guide.

Proofread these words and decide which spelling in each pair is correct. Circle the word that is correctly spelled. Then write the correct spelling of each Spelling Word.

1. reform
   riform

2. respiration
   respieration

3. fromation
   formation

4. insperation
   inspiration

5. enspired
   inspired

6. convention
   convintion

PROOFREADING 7–12. Read the following label. Circle the misspelled words. Then write the words correctly on the lines.

At last! A formulia for making yourself invisible! This mixture is simple to prepare and will fill the most tedious life with aventure. The success of the mixture depens on combining several substances until a unaform color is achieved. Instructions for antidote to come later. CAUTION: The inventer of this product has not been seen since he first swallowed the substance. Pendding his reappearance, the effectiveness of the antidote cannot be guaranteed.

FUN WITH WORDS Use Spelling Words to replace 13–16.

MR. SHUMAN'S LATEST 13 MAKES IT POSSIBLE FOR HIM TO WALK ON THE CEILING.

THIS NEW WAY OF GETTING AROUND HAS TOTALLY 14 HIS WAY OF LOOKING AT THINGS, AND HIS RUG HARDLY EVER NEEDS VACUUMING.

SOME EVERYDAY TASKS ARE MORE INTERESTING FOR MR. SHUMAN TO 15 NOW. HE ENJOYS THE CHALLENGE OF EATING WHILE 16 FROM THE CEILING.

1. _____
2. _____
3. _____
4. _____
5. _____
6. _____
7. _____
8. _____
9. _____
10. _____
11. _____
12. _____
13. _____
14. _____
15. _____
16. _____

Lesson 35: Noun Suffixes

Spelling Words

1. artist
2. pioneer
3. librarian
4. goalie
5. civilian
6. historian
7. guardian
8. scientist
9. biologist
10. volunteer
11. musician
12. engineer
13. physician
14. technician
15. politician
16. psychiatrist

Your Own Words

Look for other words with these suffixes. You might see *guitarist* or *pianist* on notes that accompany a CD or a tape. You might include *cyclist* or *pedestrian* in a description of a street scene.

17. _____
18. _____
19. _____
20. _____

Each Spelling Word ends in the suffix *-ist, -eer, -ian,* or *-ie.* When one of these suffixes is added to a base word, it often changes the meaning of the word to "one who makes or does something."

As you look at each word, identify the base word to which each suffix has been added. Then sort the Spelling Words into groups.

-IST

_____
_____
_____
_____

-IAN

_____
_____
_____
_____
_____

-EER

_____
_____
_____

-IE-

_____

The spelling of the base word sometimes changes when the suffix *-ist, -eer, -ie,* or *-ian* is added, as in *science/scientist,* and *library/librarian.*

Lesson 35: Noun Suffixes (continued)

SPELLING CLUES: Words with Suffixes Look carefully at words with suffixes. First make sure you have spelled the suffixes correctly. Then determine whether any spelling changes are required in the base word.

Proofread these words and decide which spelling in each pair is correct. Circle the word that is correctly spelled. Then write the correct spelling of each Spelling Word.

1. politician	3. guardian	5. civilian
politition	gardian	civilin
2. biolagist	4. engeneer	6. sientist
biologist	engineer	scientist

1. _____
2. _____
3. _____
4. _____
5. _____
6. _____

PROOFREADING 7–10. Proofread the following sentences. Circle the misspelled word in each sentence. Then write the words correctly on the lines.

- The technican checked the laboratory equipment and the list of procedures.
- Sometimes the goalee slides on his stomach or back to block the puck.
- The artest created huge metal sculptures.
- John Roebling was a pionneer in the design of suspension bridges.

7. _____
8. _____
9. _____
10. _____

WORKING WITH MEANING Read these Help Wanted ads. Write Spelling Words to replace 11–16.

WANTED: For summer concert program, experienced __11__ who plays banjo or guitar.

WANTED: An enthusiastic __12__ to donate five hours a week tutoring young children.

IMMEDIATE OPENING: Part-time teaching job for __13__ with background in early Asian civilizations.

NORTH COUNTY has position for trained __14__ to join staff of community mental health center.

SUMMER JOB: __15__ to help shelve and catalog children's books and tapes.

WANTED: Valley Clinic seeking __16__ interested in practicing family medicine in rural area.

11. _____
12. _____
13. _____
14. _____
15. _____
16. _____

Unit 6 Review
Practice Test: Part A

Read each sentence. Mark the circle to tell whether the underlined word is spelled correctly or incorrectly.

EXAMPLE: She picked a honeycomb from the forest.

1. Alexander Graham Bell is known for his invention of the telephone.
   correct   incorrect

2. The scientist uses a microskope to study bacteria.
   correct   incorrect

3. With the widespread use of computers today, office tecnology is greatly improved.
   correct   incorrect

4. The organization my father works for grants scholarships to students who have high grades.
   correct   incorrect

5. The libraryan helped me find the proper reference materials to complete my report.
   correct   incorrect

6. I hope to take a course in psychology when I'm in high school.
   correct   incorrect

7. Did you receive the latest computer catologue?
   correct   incorrect

8. It takes a great deal of logic to solve some math problems.
   correct   incorrect

9. The new teacher asked for our coperation.
   correct   incorrect

10. I am interested in learning about advances made in the agricultural field.
    correct   incorrect

	EXAMPLE	
	Correct	Incorrect
	⬤	◯

	ANSWERS	
1	◯	◯
2	◯	◯
3	◯	◯
4	◯	◯
5	◯	◯
6	◯	◯
7	◯	◯
8	◯	◯
9	◯	◯
10	◯	◯

Unit 6 Review (continued)
Practice Test: Part B

Read each sentence. Fill in the letter of the correctly spelled word.

EXAMPLE: The paper _____.
A riped   B ripped   C rippd   D ript

ANSWERS

1. He _____ on you for everything.
   A depens   B dependes   C depenes   D depends

   1 Ⓐ Ⓑ Ⓒ Ⓓ

2. I am interested in the works of the _____ Monet.
   A artest   B artist   C artust   D artast

   2 Ⓐ Ⓑ Ⓒ Ⓓ

3. She was a _____ in the field of medicine.
   A pioneer   B pioner   C pionear   D pionere

   3 Ⓐ Ⓑ Ⓒ Ⓓ

4. He often looks in the _____ for information.
   A encyclopia   C encyclopadia
   B encyclapedia   D encyclopedia

   4 Ⓐ Ⓑ Ⓒ Ⓓ

5. There is a strong _____ that we will soon be moving.
   A possibility   C posibility
   B possability   D possibilty

   5 Ⓐ Ⓑ Ⓒ Ⓓ

6. Can you tell me the _____ for water?
   A formila   B formule   C formulah   D formula

   6 Ⓐ Ⓑ Ⓒ Ⓓ

7. The speaker _____ us to begin recycling.
   A inspired   B inspirad   C inspyred   D inspyrd

   7 Ⓐ Ⓑ Ⓒ Ⓓ

8. In _____ class, she is learning about blood types.
   A byology   B byalogy   C biolagy   D biology

   8 Ⓐ Ⓑ Ⓒ Ⓓ

9. When I look through a _____, I can see many stars.
   A telscope   B telescop   C telescope   D telscap

   9 Ⓐ Ⓑ Ⓒ Ⓓ

10. The chorus is going to _____ on Friday.
    A preform   B perfarm   C purform   D perform

   10 Ⓐ Ⓑ Ⓒ Ⓓ

Unit 6 Review (continued)
Activities

What's in a Word?

◆ *encyclopedia*

The word *encyclopedia* is related to the word *circle*, even though its present meaning would not seem to indicate this. The original meaning of *encyclopedia* was "a circle of learning, a general education." The sense of *encyclopedia* as a book comes from the idea that it gives a full circle, or range, of information.

◆ *periscope*

The word *periscope* consists of two Greek word parts: *peri-*, meaning "around," and *-scop-*, meaning "see." A *periscope* is an instrument that provides a view all around, or on all sides.

Remember Your Roots

Do this activity with a partner or in a small group. Write the Greek word parts —*hydr-*, *-log-*, *-ology*, and *-scop-* on a set of cards. Each player should have a piece of paper and a pencil. One player should select one of the word-parts cards and place it face up. Then all the players have one minute to list as many words as they can think of that are based on the word part shown. Each correctly spelled word earns one point. Continue until the four cards have been used. Then tally up the points to determine the winner.

Pair Off for Practice

Work with a partner to make flash cards for all the Spelling Words. Place the cards face down, and take turns picking a card and pronouncing the word for your partner to spell. When a player spells a word correctly, he or she gets to keep the card. If a word is incorrectly spelled, it must be returned to the pile. Continue the practice until all the words have been correctly spelled. The partner with the most cards wins the practice match.

YOUR WORD HISTORIES

Have you kept up your collection of etymologies? Give it a twist by creating a section of Latin roots and Greek roots found in the Spelling Words and in other words you notice in your reading. Add these to your dictionary as well. Keep separate pages for words from Latin and from Greek.

◆ This indicates a Unit Spelling Word.

Unit 6 Review (continued)
Activities

Challenge Yourself

Choose eight Spelling Words that you find especially challenging. Write the definition of each word, using your own words or a dictionary definition, on a separate card. Be sure not to write the word itself. Then go through your cards, writing the word that matches each definition. On each card, write a sentence using the word.

Proofreading Partners

Do this activity with a partner. Each of you should make a list of five Spelling Words that give you trouble or that you consider the most challenging in the unit. Exchange lists. Each partner should write a paragraph using your partner's five Spelling Words, but misspelling them. Then exchange papers, and proofread and correct each other's paragraphs. Be sure each Spelling Word is spelled correctly.

Synonym Spell-Check

Work with a partner to review some of your Spelling Words. Think of synonyms for four Spelling Words. Give your partner each synonym in turn, and ask him or her to identify and then spell the Spelling Word.

What's in a Word?

philanthropic

Philanthropic people or organizations seek to help other people. They use their own money to improve the education, health, or welfare of others. The word *philanthropic* comes from the Greek *philos*, meaning "loving," combined with *anthropos*, meaning "man" or "human being." A *philanthropist*, therefore, is one who loves his or her fellow human beings.

◆ psychiatrist / psychology

The words *psychiatrist* and *psychology* are unusual words in that they begin with the letters **ps** but have the sound of "sigh." These words come from the name **Psyche,** a goddess of ancient Greece. Psyche was a princess who was thought to represent the human soul or spirit. Her name was given to studies of the human mind or human nature.

radiologist

A *radiologist* is a specialist in using X-rays and other forms of radiology. Do you wonder why the word *radio* is part of *radiologist*? In Latin, *radius* means "ray"—a beam of light or other kind of energy. The waves of electric impulses that radios receive and send are related to the high-energy waves that radiologists study.

◆ This indicates a Unit Spelling Word.

Spelling Dictionary

This is the entry word. It's the word you look up.

These marks indicate the primary and secondary accents.

Look here to find out how to pronounce the entry word.

Here you'll find other forms of the entry word, such as the plural.

This abbreviation tells what part of speech the entry word is.*

This is a sample sentence using the entry word.

met·a·mor·pho·sis [met´ə·môr´fə·sis] *n.,* **metamorphoses** 1. In lower animals, a series of complete changes in body form that take place from birth to the adult stage. 2. A complete or very obvious change: **We watched the *metamorphosis* of the tadpole into a frog.** *syns.* change, transformation [4]

These are two definitions of the entry word.

This is the number of the lesson where you'll find the entry word.

Synonyms of the word are listed right after *syn.*

Use this key to help you figure out the sounds of the letters.

Pronunciation Key

a	add, map	m	move, seem	u	up, done
ā	ace, rate	n	nice, tin	û(r)	burn, term
â(r)	care, air	ng	ring, song	yōō	fuse, few
ä	palm, father	o	odd, hot	v	vain, eve
b	bat, rub	ō	open, so	w	win, away
ch	check, catch	ô	order, jaw	y	yet, yearn
d	dog, rod	oi	oil, boy	z	zest, muse
e	end, pet	ou	pout, now	zh	vision, pleasure
ē	equal, tree	ŏŏ	took, full	ə	the schwa, an
f	fit, half	ōō	pool, food		unstressed vowel
g	go, log	p	pit, stop		representing the
h	hope, hate	r	run, poor		sound spelled
i	it, give	s	see, pass		a in about
ī	ice, write	sh	sure, rush		e in listen
j	joy, ledge	t	talk, sit		i in pencil
k	cool, take	th	thin, both		o in melon
l	look, rule	th	this, bathe		u in circus

*Key to Abbreviations: *n.* noun; *v.* verb; *adj.* adjective; *adv.* adverb; *prep.* preposition; *pron.* pronoun; *interj.* interjection; *conj.* conjunction; *syn.* synonym

Spelling Table

The sound	in	is spelled as—	The sound	in	is spelled as—
a	add	cat, laugh, plaid	ō	open	oh, over, go, oak, grow, toe, though, soul, sew
ā	age	game, rain, day, gauge	ô	dog	for, more, roar, ball, walk, dawn, fault, broad, ought
ä	palm	ah, father, dark, heart			
â(r)	care	dare, fair, prayer, where, bear, their	oi	oil	noise, toy
b	bat	big, cabin, rabbit	o͝o	took	foot, would, wolf, pull
ch	check	chop, march, catch, nature, mention	o͞o	pool	cool, lose, soup, through, rude, due, fruit, drew, canoe
d	dog	dig, bad, ladder, called			
e	egg	end, met, ready, any, said, says, friend, bury, guess	ou	out	ounce, now, bough
			p	put	pin, cap, happy
ē	equal	she, eat, see, people, key, field, machine, receive, piano, city	r	run	red, car, hurry, wrist, rhyme
			s	see	sit, scene, loss, listen, city, psychology
f	fit	five, offer, cough, half, photo	sh	rush	shoe, sure, ocean, special, machine, mission, lotion, pension, conscience
g	go	gate, bigger, vague, ghost			
h	hot	hope, who	t	top	tan, kept, better, walked, caught
i	it	inch, hit, pretty, employ, been, busy, guitar, damage, women, myth, here, dear	th	thin	think, cloth
			th	this	these, clothing
ī	ice	item, fine, pie, high, buy, try, dye, eye, height, island, aisle	u	up	cut, butter, some, flood, does, young
			û(r)	burn	turn, bird, work, early, journey, herd
j	joy	jump, gem, magic, cage, edge, soldier, graduate, exaggerate	v	very	vote, over, of
			w	win	wait, power
			y	yet	year, onion
k	keep	king, cat, lock, chorus, account	yo͞o	use	cue, few, youth, view, beautiful
l	look	let, ball			
m	move	make, hammer, calm, climb, condemn	z	zoo	zebra, lazy, buzz, was, scissors
			zh	vision	pleasure, garage, television
n	nice	new, can, funny, know, gnome, pneumonia			
ng	ring	thing, sink, tongue	ə		about, listen, pencil, melon, circus
o	odd	pot, honor			

A

ac·cel·er·ate [ak·sel´ə·rāt´] *v.* **1.** to increase in speed: **When you step on the gas pedal, a car** *accelerates.* **2.** to cause to happen sooner; to speed up: **She** *accelerated* **her studies by doing extra work.** [10]

ac·cel·er·a·tion [ak·sel´ə·rā´shən] *n.* the process of increasing in speed: **Warm, moist conditions cause the** *acceleration* **of decay.** [33]

ac·cent [ak´sent] *n.* **1.** the extra force or emphasis given to a spoken word or syllable, or the mark used to indicate such emphasis: **In pronouncing the word "accept," place the** *accent* **on the second syllable. 2.** a way of pronouncing words that is characteristic of a particular region or country: **Jean-Luke, who just moved here from Paris, speaks with a French** *accent.* **3.** emphasis: **In my family, the** *accent* **is on cooperation.** [10]

ac·cept [ak·sept´] *v.* **1.** to receive something that is offered, such as a gift, award, or invitation: **They** *accepted* **our invitation to stay for the night. 2.** to agree to: **Both countries** *accepted* **the terms of the cease-fire agreement.** [10]

ac·com·mo·date [ə·kom´ə·dāt´] *v.* **1.** to have or make room for; to provide a place to stay or sleep: **This hotel room can** *accommodate* **four people. 2.** to do a favor for: **I'd** *accommodate* **you, but I have an appointment and can't give you a ride home.** [10]

ac·com·pa·ny [ə·kum´pə·nē] *v.* to come or go along with someone or something else: **Will a parent or teacher** *accompany* **your class on the field trip?** *syn.* escort [10]

ac·com·plish [ə·kom´plish] *v.* to carry out or complete: **I can** *accomplish* **the task asked of me, but I need some supplies.** [10]

ac·cu·mu·la·tion [ə·kyoom´yə·lā´shən] *n.* something that has been gathered together: **There has been an** *accumulation* **of four feet of snow since the blizzard began.** [33]

ad·jec·tive [aj´ik·tiv] *n.* a word that modifies a noun or pronoun: **In the sentence "The purple sweater is mine,"** *purple* **is an** *adjective.* [29]

ad·min·is·tra·tion [ad·min´is·trā´shən] *n.* the act of managing or governing: **The** *administration* **of her company is very efficient.** [33]

ad·mit [ad·mit´] *v.* **1.** to confess or acknowledge: **She** *admits* **that she made a mistake.** **2.** to allow to enter: **This ticket** *admits* **one student to the performance.** [22]

ad·ven·ture [ad·ven´chər] *n.* **1.** a dangerous or difficult undertaking: **He said he climbed mountains simply for the** *adventure.* **2.** a thrilling or unusual experience: **I had quite an** *adventure* **when I visited the theme park.** [34]

ad·ver·tise [ad´vər·tīz´] *v.* to make known publicly: **To sell our product we will** *advertise* **widely.** [18]

ad·vise [ad·vīz´] *v.* to suggest a course of action; to give advice to: **I'd** *advise* **you to review your notes carefully before the quiz.** [20]

Af·ri·ca [af´ri·kə] *n.* the continent south of Europe, between the Atlantic and Indian Oceans: **The Nile River in** *Africa* **is the longest river in the world.** [9]

Af·ri·can [af´ri·kən] **1.** *adj.* having to do with the people or culture of Africa: **Bantu is an** *African* **language. 2.** *n.* a native or citizen of an African country: **My friend, Nell, is the only** *African* **I know from Johannesburg.** [9]

ag·ri·cul·tur·al [ag´rə·kul´chər·əl] *adj.* having to do with farming: **Jake wants to take over his family's farm, so he went to an** *agricultural* **college in Texas.** [33]

al·li·ga·tor [al´ə·gā´tər] *n.* a large reptile with sharp teeth and strong jaws: **The snout of an** *alligator* **is not as pointed as that of a crocodile.** [4]

a·nal·o·gy [ə·nal´ə·jē] *n.* a comparison in which two seemingly unrelated things are shown to be similar in some way: **An** *analogy* **can be made between the human brain and a computer's memory.** [32]

an·a·lyze [an´ə·līz´] *v.* to find out what something is like by separating it into parts; to examine closely: **The skater watched video tapes of her past performance and** *analyzed* **her mistakes.** [18]

an·nounce [ə·nouns´] *v.* to make known publicly or officially: **The winner of the contest will be** *announced* **next Friday.** [10]

an·noy [ə·noi´] *v.* to bother or irritate: **Does the sound of the TV** *annoy* **you when you are studying?** [10]

an·tique [an tēk´] *n.* something that was made very long ago, often especially valuable because of its age: **That** *antique* **is from the late 1800s.** [23]

a·pol·o·gize [ə·pol´ə·jīz´] *v.*, **apologizing** to say that one is sorry for some error or action, to express regret: **I** *apologized* **to Seth for interrupting him.** [32]

ap·point [ə·point´] *v.* to select for a particular duty or office: **The governor announced that he would** *appoint* **a special committee to look into the questionable situation.** [10]

ap·proach [ə·prōch´] *v.* to come near to: **The plane is** *approaching* **the runway, and I am getting nervous about taking off in the snow.** [10]

ap·prove [ə·prōōv´] *v.* to think that something is good or right: **I** *approve* **of your decision to study Spanish next year.** [10]

arc·tic [är(k)´tik] *n.* **1.** the region around the North Pole: **The** *Arctic* **has no snow or ice in the summer months. 2.** *adj.* very cold; freezing: **Alaska and many areas of Canada have** *arctic* **temperatures for more than four months of the year.** [12]

ar·range [ə·rānj´] *v.* **1.** to place in a certain way: **I** *arranged* **the flowers in a large vase. 2.** to plan or prepare for: **I'm** *arranging* **for Tim to drive you to the airport.** [10]

ar·range·ments [ə·rānj´mənts] *n.* plans or preparations: **A travel agent made all the** *arrangements* **for our trip to Hawaii.** [10]

ar·ray [ə·rā´] *n.* **1.** an orderly arrangement: **The cadets were lined up in military** *array.* **2.** a vast collection: **People came from all over to see the** *array* **of crown jewels.** [10]

ar·rest [ə·rest´] *v.* **1.** to take into custody by legal authority: **The rookie police officer** *arrested* **his primary suspect. 2.** to stop suddenly: **Can fluids and vitamin C** *arrest* **a cold? 3.** to attract and hold: **Barry waved his arms and** *arrested* **someone's attention.** [10]

ar·rive [ə·rīv´] *v.* **1.** to reach a destination: **Their train** *arrived* **at 2:45 P.M. 2.** to be at hand: **The day of the exam** *arrived* **all too soon.** [10]

ar·tist [är´tist] *n.* a person who is skilled in one of the arts, such as painting, music, literature, or dancing: **Pablo Picasso was a great** *artist* **whose style has been imitated by many other** *artists.* [35]

as·pi·rin [as´pər·in] *n.* a kind of medicine that lowers fever and reduces pain: *Aspirin* **is usually taken in the form of a tablet.** [29]

as·tro·naut [as´trə·nôt´] *n.* a person who travels in space or who navigates a spacecraft: **John Glenn was the first American** *astronaut* **to orbit the earth.** [27]

as·tron·o·mer [ə·stron´ə·mər] *n.* a person who studies astronomy: **The** *astronomer* **pointed out Saturn and Jupiter to everyone at the planetarium.** [27]

as·tron·o·my [ə·stron´ə·mē] *n.* the science that deals with stars, planets, comets, galaxies, and other bodies in space: *Astronomy* **began in ancient times and is one of the oldest sciences.** [27]

ath·lete [ath´lēt´] *n.* a person who has a skill in sports or physical exercise: *Athletes* **from all over the world compete in the Olympic Games.** [29]

at·ten·dance [ə·ten´dəns] *n.* **1.** the act of being present: **Your** *attendance* **at the assembly is required. 2.** the number of people present: **The** *attendance* **at the football game was over 85,000.** [21]

at·ti·tude [at´ə·t(y)ōōd´] *n.* a way of thinking or feeling; a point of view: **Food servers get good tips when they give restaurant patrons excellent service and have a friendly** *attitude.* [15]

at·tract [ə·trakt´] *v.* to get the interest or attention of; draw toward oneself or itself by some force or action: **A bright light will often** *attract* **insects at night.** [22]

Aus·tral·ia [ôs´trāl´yə] *n.* the continent that is southeast of Asia between the Pacific and Indian Oceans: *Australia* **is the sixth-largest country in the world and the smallest continent in the world.** [9]

• •

Pronunciation Key

a	add	ō	open	th	thin
ā	ace	ô	off	th	this
â(r)	care	oi	oil	zh	vision
ä	palm	ŏŏ	took		
e	end	ōō	pool	ə	a in about
ē	equal	ou	out		e in listen
i	it	u	up		i in pencil
ī	ice	û(r)	burn		o in melon
o	odd	yōō	use		u in circus

• •

Aus·tral·ian [ôs´trāl´yən] **1.** *adj.* having to do with the people or culture of Australia: **The** *Australian* **countryside can be dramatic. 2.** *n.* a native or citizen of Australia: **The** *Australian* **knew what a kangaroo ate because his family had raised one.** [9]

au·to·bi·og·ra·phy [ô´tə·bī·og´rə·fē] *n.* the story of a person's own life: **Ben Franklin's account of his own life was the first important American** *autobiography.* [33]

au·to·graph [ô´tə·graf´] *n.* a person's own signature: **The fans waited outside the dressing room to get the star's** *autograph.* [27]

au·to·mo·bile [ô´tə·mə·bēl´] *n.* a four-wheeled vehicle that carries passengers and is usually powered by a gasoline engine: **The use of the** *automobile* **has changed life in most countries.** *syn.* car [30]

au·tumn [ô´təm] *n.* the season of the year that comes between summer and winter: **In** *autumn* **the leaves change to brilliant reds, yellows, and oranges.** *syn.* fall [25]

au·tum·nal [ô·tum´nəl] *adj.* of or having to do with autumn: **Since it's January, this** *autumnal* **weather is very odd.** [25]

awe·some [ô´səm] *adj.* causing a feeling of fear, wonder, and respect, usually due to size or strength: **The Grand Canyon is truly an** *awesome* **sight.** [11]

awk·ward [ôk´wərd] *adj.* **1.** not graceful: **She's been practicing, but she made an** *awkward* **move.** *syn.* clumsy **2.** difficult or embarrassing: **There was an** *awkward* **silence at the dinner table after he asked a question.** [11]

B

back·ward [bak´wərd] *adv.* toward the back; in reverse order: **Mark can say the alphabet** *backward* **as fast as he can say it in the usual way.** [11]

bak·er·y [bak´(ə)rē] *n.* a place where baked goods such as bread, cake, and cookies are prepared and sold: **The delicious smell in the** *bakery* **always makes me hungry.** [14]

bal·ance [bal´əns] **1.** *n.* a condition in which two opposing items or forces are equal, as in strength, weight or value: **Some people haven't figured out how to achieve a** *balance* **between work and play. 2.** *v.* to keep one's body in a desired position without

falling: **I** *balanced* **unsteadily on the new ice skates.** [21]

bal·let [bal´ā´ *or* ba·lā´] *n.* a kind of dance characterized by flowing, graceful movement: **Dancers of** *ballet* **use formal steps and positions.** [23]

ban·jo [ban´jō] *n.* a musical instrument that is similar to a guitar: **A** *banjo* **has a small, round body; a long neck; and four or five strings.** [5]

ba·rom·e·ter [bə·rom´ə·tər] *n.* an instrument that measures air pressure and is widely used to forecast the weather: **If a** *barometer* **shows a drop in air pressure, a storm is probably on the way.** [27]

bar·ri·er [bar´ē·ər] *n.* anything that blocks the way, stops movement, or separates: **A** *barrier* **was put up to keep cars away from that street while the traffic signals were being repaired.** [15]

berth [bûrth] *n.* **1.** a space for sleeping on a train or ship: **She slept in an upper** *berth* **during her train trip across the country. 2.** a space at a wharf where a ship may dock: **The liner pulled into its** *berth* **to unload its passengers and cargo.** [2]

bev·er·age [bev´rij *or* bev´ər·ij] *n.* a drink: **Orange juice is a** *beverage* **that people often drink at breakfast.** [12]

bi·cy·cle [bī´sik·əl] *n.* a vehicle with two large wheels, one behind the other: **Mom exercises every day on a stationary** *bicycle.* [28]

bin·oc·u·lars [bə·nok´yə·lərz] *n.* two short telescopes that are fastened together so that a person can view distant objects with both eyes: **Our seats are in the top row of the stadium, so we'll need** *binoculars* **to help us see the field more clearly.** [28]

bi·og·ra·phy [bī·og´rə·fē] *n.* the story of a person's life: **Last week we watched a TV special—a** *biography* **of President John Kennedy.** [27]

bi·ol·o·gist [bī·ol´ə·jist] *n.* a person who studies or is an expert in biology: **Andrea is taking several science courses so that she can become a** *biologist.* [35]

bi·ol·o·gy [bī·ol´ə·jē] *n.* the science that deals with living things and their growth, development, and reproduction: **Botany and zoology are two branches of** *biology.* [32]

birth [bûrth] *n.* **1.** the act or fact of being born: **Jack's relatives celebrated his** *birth.* **2.** the beginning of something: **The Declaration of Independence in 1776 represents the** *birth* **of the United States.** *syn.* origin [2]

both·er [both´ər] *v.* to annoy or irritate: **When my sister stops** *bothering* **me, I will study.** [3]

bound·a·ry [boun´də·rē *or* boun´drē] *n.* the outer limit or edge of something: **A fence marks the** *boundary* **of their property.** [12]

bou·quet [bō·ka´ *or* boo·ka´] *n.* **1.** a bunch of flowers: **We sent a** *bouquet* **of roses to Grandma on Mother's Day. 2.** a delicate fragrance or aroma: **The apricot nectar had a pleasant** *bouquet.* [23]

bril·liant [bril´yənt] *adj.* **1.** very bright or vivid: **The** *brilliant* **sunshine felt wonderful on our faces. 2.** extremely intelligent: **Jenna is a** *brilliant* **student. 3.** splendid; magnificent: **I thought our dance troupe put on a** *brilliant* **performance.** [21]

buf·fa·lo [buf´ə·lō] *n.* an animal that is similar to an ox, with a large, round body and curved horns: **In many movies about the old West,** *buffalo* **roam the plains.** [15]

buf·fet [boo·fā´] *n.* **1.** a meal at which the guests serve themselves from stationary platters of food: **At a** *buffet,* **you can usually serve yourself as much and as often as you like. 2.** a piece of furniture with drawers and shelves for storing silver, glassware, or table linens: **We keep our good china in the** *buffet* **in the dining room.** [23]

bu·gle [byoo´gəl] *n.* a kind of small trumpet without valves, used to sound a call, especially in the armed forces: **"Reveille" and "Taps" are calls played on the** *bugle.* [5]

C

caf·e·te·ri·a [kaf´ə·tir´ē·ə] *n.* a restaurant in which customers select and pay for food at a counter and then carry it to their tables for eating: **At a** *cafeteria,* **foods are usually set out in individual servings.** [4]

cal·cu·late [kal´kyə·lāt´] *v.* to figure using mathematics: **She will** *calculate* **our scores on the test by multiplying the number of correct answers by four.** [18]

cam·ou·flage [kam´ə·fläzh´] *n.* certain materials used to change the appearance of something,

in order to hide or protect it: **The soldiers wore** *camouflage* **to protect themselves in the jungle.** [23]

car·a·van [kar´ə·van´] *n.* **1.** a group of traders or pilgrims traveling together, as through a desert: **We could see the** *caravan* **of camels approaching slowly across the desert. 2.** a covered wagon or truck used as a house on wheels: **The early settlers traveled west in** *caravans.* [30]

car·bo·hy·drate [kär´bō·hī´drāt´] *n.* any of a group of chemical compounds consisting of carbon, hydrogen, and oxygen that are made by plants during photosynthesis: **Sugar is one kind of** *carbohydrate.* [32]

car·ry [kar´ē] *v.* to transport from one place to another: **The truck was** *carrying* **a load of fruit to the city.** [3]

cat·a·log [kat´ə·lôg´ *or* kat´ə·log´] *n.* a list of things for sale or for use, often including descriptions: **Many people shop for clothes through mail-order** *catalogs.* [32]

cel·e·brate [sel´ə·brāt´] *v.* to mark an event or occasion in a special way: **We'll** *celebrate* **your birthday by going out to dinner.** [18]

cen·ti·me·ter [sen´tə·mē´tər] *n.* a unit of length that is equal to one-hundredth of a meter: **There are about 2.54** *centimeters* **in 1 inch.** [27]

cen·tu·ry [sen´chə·rē] *n.* a period of one hundred years: **During the twentieth** *century,* **there were two world wars.** [14]

chair·per·son [châr´pûr´sən] *n.* a person who is in charge of a meeting or is the head of a committee: **The** *chairperson* **called the meeting to order.** [1]

• •

Pronunciation Key

a	add	ō	open	th	thin
ā	ace	ô	off	th	this
â(r)	care	oi	oil	zh	vision
ä	palm	oŏ	took		
e	end	oō	pool	ə	a in about
ē	equal	ou	out		e in listen
i	it	u	up		i in pencil
ī	ice	û(r)	burn		o in melon
o	odd	yoō	use		u in circus

• •

cham·pi·on [cham´pē·ən] **1.** *n.* someone or something that is better than all the other competitors, as in a sport or contest: **I'm so proud our daughter is the school's spelling** *champion.* **2.** *v.* to fight for a person or a cause: **My father will always** *champion* **the cause of freedom.** [30]

char·ac·ter·is·tic [kar´ik·tə·ris´tik] **1.** *adj.* showing the nature of something: **White is the** *charac-teristic* **color of a polar bear.** *syn.* typical. **2.** *n.* a special quality: **Generosity is a** *charac-teristic* **of people who give money to charity.** *syn.* trait [33]

cheat [chēt] *v.* to act unfairly or dishonestly: **The teacher stayed in the room during the exam to be sure that no one was** *cheating.* [3]

child·ish [chīl´dish] *adj.* in the manner of or proper for a child, but inappropriate for an adult: **No one thought Jeff's** *childish* **behav-ior was funny, especially since he's 33 years old.** *syn.* immature [11]

chil·i [chil´ē] *n.* a sharp-tasting spice that comes from a kind of red pepper: **Food with** *chili* **in it makes my eyes water.** [4]

choc·o·late [chôk´(ə·)lit *or* chok´(ə·)lit] *n.* a food product made of ground cacao beans, used in candies and in baking: **The usual color of** *chocolate* **is brown.** [29]

chute [shōot] *n.* a vertical or sloping passage through which things can be dropped or passed: **The only chore I still have to do is gathering dirty clothes and throwing them down the laundry** *chute.* [2]

cin·na·mon [sin´ə·mən] *n.* an aromatic reddish-brown spice that comes from the bark of a tropical tree: *Cinnamon* **is used as a flavoring in apple pie.** [15]

cir·cle [sûr´kəl] *n.* **1.** a closed, flat curve on which every point is equally distant from a point at the center: *Circles* **are geometric figures. 2.** anything that has this round shape: **I was dizzy from turning around and around in** *circles.* [16]

cir·cu·lar [sûr´ kyə·lər] **1.** *adj.* shaped like a circle; continuously curving: **My favorite part of the house was the** *circular* **staircase. 2.** *n.* a letter or advertisement that is distrib-uted to many people: **The new restaurant sent out a** *circular* **in the Sunday paper to announce its grand opening.** [16]

ci·vil·ian [sə·vil´yən] **1.** *adj.* not having to do with or belonging to the armed forces: **A soldier who is off duty can change out of his or her uniform into** *civilian* **clothes. 2.** *n.* a person who is not a member of the armed forces: **During the war, many** *civilians* **worked in defense plants.** [35]

clar·i·net [klar´ə·net´] *n.* a woodwind instru-ment with a high-pitched tone: **The** *clarinet* **has a narrow body with a flared end.** [5]

clas·si·cal [klas´i·kəl] *adj.* **1.** having to do with ancient Roman and Greek culture: **Most of her paintings depict a** *classical* **style of architecture. 2.** following a strict, established form: **Jenny's mother wants her to study** *classical* **music.** [5]

co·coa [kō´kō] *n.* a brown powder made from cacao beans, or a drink made from this powder: **A cup of hot** *cocoa* **tastes good on a cold day.** [4]

co·lo·ni·al [kə·lō´nē·əl] *adj.* having to do with a colony or colonies, especially the thirteen original American colonies: **Life in** *colonial* **America was different from life today.** [24]

col·o·ny [kol´ə·nē] *n.* a group of people who settle in a distant land but are ruled by the government of their native country: **Massachusetts was a British** *colony* **before it became part of the United States.** [24]

com·mit·ment [kə·mit´mənt] *n.* a pledge or obligation: **The basketball player made a** *commitment* **to finish college before turning professional.** [22]

com·pan·ion [kəm·pan´yən] *n.* a person who associates with or goes along with another: **On the quiz show, she won a trip to Hawaii for herself and a** *companion.* *syn.* comrade [24]

com·pa·ny [kum´pə·nē] *n.* **1.** a group of people who join together to do business: **My friend loves her co-workers at the telephone** *com-pany.* **2.** someone who comes to visit; a guest or guests: **We usually eat in the dining room when we have** *company.* [24]

com·pel [kəm·pel´] *v.,* **compelled** to force an action: **The prisoners were** *compelled* **to march quickly in single file.** [3]

com·pos·er [kəm·pō´zər] *n.* a person who makes up or creates something, especially music: **Johann Sebastian Bach is a famous** *composer.* [5]

com·po·si·tion [kom´pə·zish´ən] *n.* **1.** the make-up of something: **The basic chemical** *compo-sition* **of water is two parts hydrogen and**

one part oxygen. **2.** something that is put together: **Mozart wrote musical** *compositions.* **3.** a short essay: **I had to write a** *composition* **for English class.** [20]

com·pro·mise [kom´prə·mīz´] *n.* an agreement between opposing sides in which each side gives up some of its demands: **The union members voted whether or not to accept the** *compromise.* [18]

con·cert [kon´sûrt] *n.* a musical performance: **Amy is singing a popular folk song at the** *concert.* [5]

con·duc·tor [kən·duk´tər] *n.* a person who leads or directs: **The** *conductor* **raised his baton, and the concert hall grew silent.** [5]

con·fi·dence [kon´fə·dəns] *n.* a feeling of trust or assurance: **Martha has** *confidence* **in her coach and follows all his suggestions.** [21]

con·grat·u·late [kən·grach´ə·lāt´] *v.* to express one's pleasure at the achievement or good fortune of another: **Everyone crowded around and** *congratulated* **him on winning the race.** [18]

con·stant [kon´stənt] *adj.* happening in an unchanging or uninterrupted way: **There was a** *constant* **sound of traffic from the nearby freeway.** [21]

con·struct [kən·strukt´] *v.* to make or build: **The city is** *constructing* **a new library near the lake.** [20]

con·tract [kən·trakt´] *v,* **1.** to make a binding agreement: **The artist** *contracted* **with the publisher to illustrate a book. 2.** to draw together and take up less space: **The metal** *contracted* **in the cold.** *syn.* shrink [22]

con·trol [kən·trōl´] *v.,* **controlling 1.** to manage or operate: **The pilot** *controlled* **the airplane in spite of the high winds. 2.** to restrain; hold back: **Kim** *controlled* **her temper more effectively after the seminar.** [3]

con·ven·tion [kən·ven´shən] *n.* **1.** the usual or accepted way of doing things: **Shaking hands when meeting someone is a** *convention* **in this country. 2.** a formal meeting for some purpose: **He will attend the booksellers'** *convention* **next month.** [34]

co·op·er·ate [kō·op´ə·rāt´] *v.* to work together for some purpose: **The witness** *cooperated* **with the police.** [18]

co·op·er·a·tion [kō·op´ə·rā´shən] *n.* assistance: **The mayor thanked his workers for their** *cooperation* **in his reelection campaign.** [33]

cor·ral [kə·ral´] *n.* a fenced area for livestock: **The cowhands rounded up the cattle and drove them into the** *corral.* [4]

cor·ri·dor [kôr´ə·dər] *n.* a narrow hallway with rooms opening onto it: **We are not supposed to run in any** *corridor* **at school.** [15]

cou·pon [k(y)ōō´pon] *n.* a ticket or advertisement that entitles the bearer to something: **If you have a** *coupon,* **our supermarket gives you credit for twice the amount.** [23]

coy·o·te [kī·ō´tē] *n.* a wolflike animal that is found in central and western North America: **A** *coyote* **has a pointed face and a bushy tail with a black tip.** [4]

crit·i·cize [krit´ə·sīz´] *v.* to find fault with; judge harshly: **If you constantly** *criticize* **my work, I'll find a new art teacher.** [18]

D

day·light [dā´līt´] *n.* sunlight; light that occurs naturally during the day: **There are more hours of** *daylight* **in summer than in winter.** [1]

dec·ade [dek´ād´] *n.* a period of ten years: **From 1990 to 2000 was a** *decade.* [28]

de·cay [di·kā´] *v.* to rot or decompose: **Brian's teeth were** *decaying* **because he was not practicing proper oral hygiene.** [8]

De·cem·ber [di·sem´bər] *n.* the twelfth month of the year: *December* **is the month that follows November.** [28]

dec·i·mal [des´ə·məl] *adj.* having to do with or based on the number 10: **A fraction with a denominator of 10 or a multiple of 10, such as 100, is called a** *decimal* **fraction.** [28]

de·cline [di·klīn´] *v.* **1.** to refuse politely: **She** *declined* **the invitation to the party because she was too busy to go. 2.** to become less numerous or strong: **Your health may** *decline* **if you don't exercise regularly.** [8]

●●●●●●●●●●●●●●●●●●●●●●●●●●●●●●●●●●●

Pronunciation Key

a	add	ō	open	th	thin
ā	ace	ô	off	th	this
â(r)	care	oi	oil	zh	vision
ä	palm	ŏŏ	took		
e	end	ōō	pool	ə	a in about
ē	equal	ou	out		e in listen
i	it	u	up		i in pencil
ī	ice	û(r)	burn		o in melon
o	odd	yōō	use		u in circus

●●●●●●●●●●●●●●●●●●●●●●●●●●●●●●●●●●●

de·duc·tion [di·duk´shən] *n.* **1.** an amount subtracted: **The judges take a *deduction* from the score for each error a performer makes. 2.** a conclusion based on reasoning, or the process of reaching such a conclusion: **I had to make a logical *deduction*.** [8]

de·feat [di·fēt´] *v.* to conquer or overcome: **The voters *defeated* the proposal.** [8]

de·fect [dē´fekt´ *or* di·fekt´] *n.* a flaw or missing element: **The studio sells pottery that isn't perfect, but the *defects* are hardly noticeable.** [8]

de·hy·drate [dē·hī´drāt´] *v.* to lose water; dry up: **The plants on the back porch had *dehydrated* in the hot sun.** [32]

de·pend [di·pend´] *v.* **1.** to trust or rely upon someone: **Mom *depends* on me to walk the dog every morning. 2.** to be determined by something else: **How quickly we finish *depends* on how soon we start and how hard we work.** [34]

de·pen·dent [di·pen´dənt] *adj.* **1.** relying on someone or something else for support: **Children are *dependent* on their parents for love and care. 2.** controlled or decided by something else: **The size of the voter turnout is *dependent* upon the weather.** [8]

de·pos·it [di·poz´it] *v.* **1.** to set down or place: **We rushed in for dinner and *deposited* our books on the table in the hall. 2.** to put down in the form of a layer: **The ocean is constantly *depositing* sand on the beach. 3.** to give over for safekeeping: **I've been *depositing* my allowance in a bank.** [20]

de·sign [di·zīn´] *v.* to create a plan for: **That house was *designed* by the famous architect Frank Lloyd Wright.** [25]

des·ig·nate [dez´ig·nāt´] *v,* **1.** to point out; indicate: **The sign *designated* the principal's office. 2.** to name or stand for: **Casey was *designated* as our class delegate to the meeting.** [25]

des·per·ate [des´pər·it] *adj.* ready to do anything because of having little hope or choice: **There is a *desperate* criminal on the run. 2.** critical or extreme: **He had a *desperate* need for money, so he begged his friend for some.** [29]

de·stroy [di·stroi´] *v.* to ruin or put an end to: **Our sand castle was *destroyed* by a huge wave.** [8]

de·struc·tion [di·struk´shən] *n.* great ruin or damage: **The tornado left a path of *destruction*.** [20]

di·a·logue [dī´ə·lôg´ *or* dī´ə·log´] *n.* **1.** a conversation between two or more people: **How can we have a *dialogue* if you won't answer me? 2.** the words spoken by characters in a story or play: **The *dialogue* for each character and the stage directions are a part of a play's script.** [23]

di·am·e·ter [dī·am´ə·tər] *n.* a straight line that passes through the center of a circle and divides the circle into two equal parts: **Draw a circle with a *diameter* of six inches.** [27]

dic·tion·ar·y [dik´shən·er´ē] *n.* a book that lists words in alphabetical order and gives information about the words, such as their meanings and pronunciations: **That *dictionary* has quotations showing how words are used by famous writers.** [14]

dif·fer·ent [dif´(ə·)rənt] *adj.* **1.** not alike: **Her taste in clothing is very *different* from her twin sister's. 2.** separate or distinct: **You'll need two *different* folders—one for homework and one for tests.** [12]

di·plo·ma·cy [di·plō´mə·sē] *n.* the management of relations between countries without going to war: **The office of Secretary of State should be filled by a person who is highly skilled in *diplomacy*.** [24]

dip·lo·mat·ic [dip´lə·mat´ik] *adj.* skillful in dealing with others: **Debra was very *diplomatic*; she told Scott what she thought without hurting his feelings.** *syns.* tactful, discreet [24]

dis·a·bled [dis·ā´bəld] *adj.* being without certain abilities: **Parking places have been provided close to stores for people who are physically *disabled*.** [8]

dis·ad·van·tage [dis´əd·van´tij] *n.* **1.** something that stands in the way of success: **His lack of education was a *disadvantage*. 2.** an unfavorable situation: **Asthma and a small cold were *disadvantages* the gymnast overcame during the competition.** [8]

dis·ap·pear [dis´ə·pir´] *v.* **1.** to pass out of sight: **The sun slowly *disappeared* below the horizon.** *syn.* vanish **2.** to pass out of existence: **Dinosaurs *disappeared* from Earth many thousands of years ago.** [8]

dis·ap·point·ment [dis´ə·point´mənt] *n.* a feeling of not having one's wishes or expectations fulfilled: **Not getting the part in the play was a tremendous *disappointment* to Suzanne.** [8]

dis·as·trous [di·zas´trəs] *adj.* causing great damage: **A *disastrous* airplane crash was the top story on last night's news.** [29]

dis·cov·er [dis·kuv´ər] *v.* to find or find out something, especially before anyone else: **Alexander Fleming *discovered* penicillin.** [8]

dis·cov·er·y [dis·kuv´ər·ē] *n.* the act of discovering, or the thing discovered: **The *discovery* of the polio vaccine prevented many people from being infected with the disease.** [14]

dis·guise [dis·gīz´] *n.* something worn by a person to conceal his or her identity: **During the Civil War, the spy went behind enemy lines wearing a *disguise.*** [8]

dis·like [dis·līk´] *v.* to feel no liking for: **I have always *disliked* scary movies.** [8]

dis·miss [dis·mis´] *v.* **1.** to get rid of or allow to leave: **The teacher *dismissed* the class. 2.** to refuse to consider: **She *dismissed* the plan even before she heard all of it.** [22]

dis·pose [dis·pōz´] *v.* **1.** to be inclined: **He was not *disposed* to believe her story. 2.** to get rid of, as by throwing away: **Please *dispose* of the can properly.** [8]

dis·solve [di·zolv´] *v.* **1.** to pass into solution or become liquid: **The sugar *dissolved* in the hot tea. 2.** to melt; fade away; vanish: **The last scene in the movie *dissolved* into the credits.** [8]

dis·tract [dis·trakt´] *v.* to draw (a person's) attention away from something else: **When Michael is at work, he wears ear plugs so that no noise will *distract* him.** [22]

doc·u·men·ta·ry [dok´yə·men´tər·ē] *adj.* based on facts or documents: **A *documentary* film interprets factual material for education or entertainment.** [14]

doubt [dout] *v.* to have a feeling of distrust or uncertainty about someone or something: **Based on his past performance, I *doubt* that he will make a good chairperson.** [17]

doubt·ful [dout´fəl] *adj.* **1.** uncertain: **A pessimist will always expect a *doubtful* outcome. 2.** questionable: **Tom, the playground bully, has acquired a *doubtful* reputation.** [17]

doubt·less [dout´ləs] *adv.* without doubt; certainly: **Fran is *doubtless* the best speller in our class.** [17]

drown [droun] *v.* to die or cause to die by suffocation in water or another liquid: **Three sailors were missing from the ship, and it was feared that they had *drowned.*** [29]

E

ec·stat·ic [ek·stat´ik] *adj.* full of great happiness: **Tammy was *ecstatic* about getting an 'A' in chemistry.** [29]

ed·i·tor [ed´i·tər] *n.* **1.** a person who improves and corrects written material to prepare it for publication: **The publishing company has an opening for a copy *editor.* 2.** a person who is in charge of a newspaper or magazine or of any of its departments: **My friend's dad is a managing *editor* for a popular teen magazine. 3.** a person who selects parts of a film, tape, or soundtrack for viewing or listening: **Jeff's dream is to become a famous film or television *editor.*** [24]

ed·i·to·ri·al [ed´i·tôr´ē·əl] **1.** *n.* an article in a newspaper or magazine that expresses the opinion of the editor or publisher: **I think the *editorial* in our evening paper is much too conservative. 2.** *adj.* having to do with an editor: **It's *editorial* policy to finish at least one chapter a day.** [24]

el·e·gant [el´ə·gənt] *adj.* showing richness, beauty, and refinement: **She wore the most *elegant* dress to the award ceremony.** *syns.* tasteful, luxurious [21]

en·close [in·klōz´] *v.* **1.** to surround; close in on all sides: **A white picket fence *encloses* the backyard. 2.** to insert something in an envelope or container along with what is being sent: **Please *enclose* a recent picture with your application.** [7]

Pronunciation Key

a	add	ō	open	th	thin
ā	ace	ô	off	t̶h̶	this
â(r)	care	oi	oil	zh	vision
ä	palm	o͝o	took		
e	end	o͞o	pool	ə	a in about
ē	equal	ou	out		e in listen
i	it	u	up		i in pencil
ī	ice	û(r)	burn		o in melon
o	odd	yo͞o	use		u in circus

en·cour·age [in·kûr´ij] *v.* **1.** to give courage or confidence to; inspire; urge: **I** *encourage* **you to apply for this job, since you seem to be well qualified. 2.** to provide favorable conditions for; help bring about: **Adding fertilizer to your plants will** *encourage* **new growth.** *syn.* foster [7]

en·cy·clo·pe·di·a [in·sī´klə·pē´dē·ə] *n.* a book or set of books that contains articles about a wide range of subjects, listed in alphabetical order: **When Bruce needs information about almost anything, he looks in the** *encyclopedia.* [33]

en·dur·ance [in·d(y)ŏŏr´əns] *n.* the ability to put up with and last through hardship or strain: **It takes a lot of** *endurance* **to be a cross-country skier.** [21]

en·gi·neer [en´jə·nir´] *n.* **1.** a person who is trained in engineering: **An** *engineer* **is involved in the planning, design, and building of complex structures and equipment. 2.** a person who operates a locomotive: **The** *engineer* **blew the train whistle as the train approached the crossroads.** [35]

Eng·land [ing´glənd] *n.* the largest division of the United Kingdom, in the southern part of the island of Great Britain: **London is the capital of** *England.* [9]

Eng·lish [ing´glish] **1.** *adj.* having to do with the people or culture of England. **The** *English* **Channel borders Great Britain on the south. 2.** *n.* the language that was first spoken in England and is now also spoken in the United States and many other countries that were once under British rule: *English* **is written from left to right.** [9]

en·joy [in·joi´] *v.* to receive pleasure or satisfaction from: **Are you** *enjoying* **your new home?** [7]

en·thu·si·asm [in·thŏŏ´zē·az´əm] *n.* great interest or keen excitement: **It was hard for the team members to keep up their** *enthusiasm* **after losing so many games.** [7]

en·ve·lope [en´və·lōp´ *or* än´və·lōp´] *n.* a paper folder with a gummed flap, used for mailing letters: **Be sure to put your return address on the** *envelope.* [7]

es·pe·cial·ly [is·pesh´əl·ē] *adv.* particularly: **She's excited about going to college,** *especially* **after winning that scholarship.** [17]

ex·am·i·na·tion [ig·zam´ə·nā´shən} *n.* **1.** the act or process of looking at something closely:

The entire track team needed a physical *examination.* **2.** a formal test of knowledge or skill: **Five of us stayed up all night to study for our final** *examination.* [30]

ex·ceed [ik·sēd´] *v.* to be greater in size, number, or scope than: **Attendance at the concert will far** *exceed* **last year's.** [7]

ex·cel [ik·sel´] *v.* to do or be better than others: **Sandy will** *excel* **in chemistry.** [7]

ex·cep·tion·al·ly [ik·sep´shən·əl·ē] *adv.* to an extraordinary or unusual degree: **Ted is** *exceptionally* **shy and rarely talks in class.** [33]

ex·change [iks·chānj´] *v.* to give and receive in return; trade one thing for something else: **When we had a car accident, we** *exchanged* **telephone numbers with the other driver for insurance purposes.** [7]

ex·cite·ment [ik·sīt´mənt] *n.* **1.** the condition of being full of strong feelings: *Excitement* **swept through the crowd as the runner neared the finish line. 2.** commotion; agitation: **In the** *excitement* **of moving, someone forgot to pack the dog's bowl.** [7]

ex·claim [iks·klām´] *v.* to say in a sudden or forceful way: **She** *exclaimed* **"Not again!" at her audition for the TV pilot.** [7]

ex·clude [iks·klŏŏd´] *v.* to leave or keep out: **The requirements for this position** *exclude* **anyone without a college degree.** [7]

ex·er·cise [ek´sər·sīz´] **1.** *v.* to move actively in order to strengthen: **Speed skaters** *exercise* **to strengthen their thigh muscles. 2.** *v.* to use or put into action: **The governor will** *exercise* **his right to veto the bill. 3.** *n.* one of a series of activities used to practice or to strengthen a skill: **There is only one review** *exercise* **at the end of this chapter in our math book.** [18]

ex·is·tence [ig·zis´təns] *n.* **1.** the act or fact of being or of being alive: **Increasing pollution may actually threaten our very** *existence.* **2.** a way of living: **Since she retired from her job, she's been leading a quiet, peaceful** *existence.* [21]

ex·it [eg´zit *or* ek´sit] *n.* a way to get out: **In case of a fire, we must all leave the building via an emergency** *exit.* [7]

ex·pand [ik·spand´] *v.* to make or become larger in size, number, or scope; take up more space: **Don't add too much rice; it will** *expand* **as it cooks.** [7]

ex·pe·ri·ence [ik·spir´ē·əns] **1.** *n.* something done or lived through: **The icestorm we had here three years ago was a frightening** *experience.* **2.** *n.* skill or knowledge gained from having done or lived through something: **Mr. Trush has ten years of** *experience* **in the oil business. 3.** *v.* to feel, live through, or participate in: **Visiting California I** *experienced* **an earthquake.** [21]

ex·plode [ik·splōd´] *v.* to break apart suddenly and violently: **The balloon** *exploded* **with a bang.** [7]

ex·press [ik·spres´] **1.** *v.* to put into words: **I wrote the Hodges and** *expressed* **my thanks. 2.** *v.* to convey without using words: **Tears** *express* **sadness. 3.** *adj.* clearly stated: **That was his** *express* **wish. 4.** *adj.* very quick: **They needed the manuscript yesterday, so I had to send it by** *express* **mail.** [7]

ex·tend [ik·stend´] *v.* **1.** to reach or stretch: *Extend* **your arms over your head. 2.** to lengthen: **The library will** *extend* **its hours on Saturdays.** [7]

F

fac·to·ry [fak´tər·ē] *n.* a building where goods are manufactured or put together: **When the auto** *factory* **closed down, many people were unemployed for a long time.** [14]

fa·mil·iar [fə·mil´yər] *adj.* well known; often seen or heard: **"Happy Birthday" is a** *familiar* **tune.** [24]

fam·i·ly [fam´ə·lē *or* fam´lē] *n.* **1.** a group of people that make up a household, often consisting of parents and their children: **My** *family* **lives in a two-story house. 2.** a group of people or things that are related in some way: **The lion belongs to the cat** *family.* [24]

fan·tas·tic [fan·tas´tik] *adj.* amazing or unbelievable: **The singers and dancers put on a** *fantastic* **performance.** [24]

fan·ta·sy [fan´tə·sē] *n.* something imagined: **The movie** *Beauty and the Beast* **is a** *fantasy.* [24]

fa·tigue [fə·tēg´] *n.* the condition of being very tired: **The singer had to cancel his tour because he was suffering from extreme** *fatigue.* [23]

Feb·ru·ar·y [feb´rŏŏ·er´ē *or* feb´yŏŏ·er´ē] *n.* the second month of the year, coming between January and March: *February* **usually has 28 days, but it has 29 days in a leap year.** [12]

fem·i·nine [fem´ə·nin] *adj.* having to do with, or typical of, the female sex: *She, her,* **and** *hers* **are in the** *feminine* **gender.** [11]

fid·dle [fid´(ə)l] *n.* an informal name for a violin: **He lifted his** *fiddle* **to his chin and began to play.** [5]

fol·low [fol´ō] *v.* to come after or behind: **We've been** *following* **the same slow car for ten minutes.** [3]

fool·ish [fŏŏ´lish] *adj.* not showing good sense: **I think she and her boyfriend sound** *foolish* **when they talk baby talk to each other.** *syn.* silly [11]

for·ma·tion [fôr·mā´shən] *n.* **1.** the act of forming: **I love to watch the** *formation* **of icicles on a window. 2.** an arrangement: **The** *formation* **the band made during half-time spelled B. H. S. for Bogota High School.** [34]

for·mu·la [fôr´myə·lə] *n.* **1.** an expression that uses symbols to show a mathematical relationship or the makeup of a chemical compound: **NaCl is the chemical** *formula* **for salt. 2.** an established way of doing or making something: **I have yet to find a** *formula* **for success.** [34]

for·tu·nate [fôr´chə·nit] *adj.* lucky: **We were** *fortunate* **to get good seats for the game.** [17]

for·tune [fôr´chən] *n.* **1.** good luck: **It's a blessing to have good** *fortune.* **2.** a large sum of money: **Repairing the roof is going to cost a** *fortune.* [17]

France [frans] *n.* a country in western Europe: **Paris is the capital of** *France.* [9]

French [french] **1.** *adj.* having to do with the people or culture of France: **In Paris, I ate all the** *French* **pastries I could get my hands on. 2.** *n.* the language that is spoken in France: **When Pierre spoke to me in** *French,* **I understood only "Bonjour."** [9]

· ·

Pronunciation Key

a	add	ō	open	th	thin
ā	ace	ô	off	th̶	this
â(r)	care	oi	oil	zh	vision
ä	palm	ŏŏ	took		
e	end	ōō	pool	ə	a in about
ē	equal	ou	out		e in listen
i	it	u	up		i in pencil
ī	ice	û(r)	burn		o in melon
o	odd	yōō	use		u in circus

· ·

fre·quent [frē´kwənt] *adj.* occurring often: **We have *frequent* rains here in the spring.** [21]

G

gal·ler·y [gal´ər·ē] *n.* **1.** a place where works of art are on display: **There is an exhibit of photos at the art *gallery*. 2.** an indoor balcony, especially the highest balcony, as in a theater or church: **We had seats in the *gallery* and could barely see the dancers.** [15]

gas·o·line [gas´ə·lēn´] *n.* a liquid that is made from petroleum and is used to fuel motors: **Most cars have engines that run on *gasoline*.** [30]

gath·er [gath´ər] *v.* to come or bring together; collect: **She *gathered* up all her notes and papers.** [3]

gen·u·ine [jen´yōō·in] *adj.* real or actual; not fake: **How can you tell if this is a *genuine* diamond?** [11]

ge·og·ra·phy [je·og´rə·fē] *n.* the study of the natural features of the earth, such as mountains and bodies of water, sometimes also including its peoples, natural resources, and climates: ***Geography* is often taught as part of social studies.** [27]

goal·ie [gō´lē] *n.* an informal word for *goalkeeper*, the player who defends the team's goal in sports such as soccer or hockey: **The *goalie* in hockey wears heavy padding on his or her legs and body.** [35]

go·ril·la [gə·ril´ə] *n.* a large, powerful ape found in the jungles of central Africa: **The *gorilla* has a broad, heavy chest and shoulders; long arms; and short legs.** [15]

grand·par·ent [gran(d)´pâr´ənt] *n.* the mother or father of a parent; a grandmother or a grandfather: **We spent Thanksgiving with our *grandparents*.** [1]

graph [graf] *n.* a kind of diagram with lines, bars, or curves that show how certain facts or numbers relate to each other: **The *graph* showed the relationship of births to deaths over a 10-year period.** [27]

gray·ish [grā´ish] *adj.* somewhat gray in color: **The sky had an odd *grayish* look.** [11]

Greece [grēs] *n.* a country in southeastern Europe that includes the southern end of the Balkan Peninsula and several islands in the Aegean Sea: **Athens is the capital of *Greece*.** [9]

Greek [grēk] **1.** *adj.* having to do with the people or culture of Greece: **The drafting class studied *Greek* architecture. 2.** *n.* a native or citizen of Greece: **John's mother is a *Greek* and his father is an Italian. 3.** *n.* the language of Greece: **Are you learning ancient or modern *Greek*?** [9]

green·ish [grēn´ish] *adj.* somewhat green in color: **The bananas were *greenish* and not yet ripe.** [11]

groan [grōn] *v.* **1.** to make a long, low sound, as in expressing pain, boredom, or despair: **He *groaned* in pain. 2.** to make a rough, creaking sound, often due to a heavy load: **The wagon wheels *groaned* as they slowly turned.** [3]

guard·i·an [gär´dē·ən] *n.* **1.** a person or thing who guards, watches over, or protects: **The Constitution is considered the *guardian* of our rights. 2.** a person appointed by the court to make personal and financial decisions for someone who is young or incompetent: **My grandmother chose her eldest son as her legal *guardian*.** [35]

gui·tar [gi·tär´] *n.* a musical instrument with strings and a pear-shaped body: **Many folk singers accompany themselves on the *guitar*.** [4]

gym·na·si·um [jim·nā´zē·əm] *n.* a large room or building where athletes train and certain sports are played: **The basketball game was held in the school *gymnasium*.** [30]

H

ham·mer [ham´ər] *v.* to pound with a hammer: **He *hammered* the nail into the board.** [3]

hand·some [han´səm] *adj.* having a pleasing appearance; good-looking: **The movie star's fans think of him as a very *handsome* man.** [11]

har·mo·ny [här´mə·nē] *n.* **1.** a pleasing combination, as of musical sounds: **The trio sang in three-part *harmony*. 2.** agreement: **Diplomats in the United Nations work to achieve *harmony* throughout the world.** [5]

harp [härp] *n.* a musical instrument with strings set on a triangular frame: **A *harp* makes a lovely sound when its strings are plucked.** [5]

haste [hāst] *n.* extreme hurry: **She left the house in some *haste* and forgot to turn off the lights.** [25]

has·ten [hāˊsən] *v.* to move swiftly or hurriedly: **They will** *hasten* **if they want to catch the beginning of the movie.** [25]

head·ache [hedˊākˊ] *n.* a dull, continuous pain in the head: **Mom had a bad** *headache* **and went to lie down for a while.** [1]

heir [âr] *n.* a person who inherits or is expected to inherit something: **The prince is** *heir* **to the throne now occupied by his father, the king.** [25]

her·i·tage [herˊə·tij] *n.* something handed down from previous generations: **The** *heritage* **of our country comes from many different cultures.** [25]

his·to·ri·an [his·tôrˊē·ən] *n.* a person who writes or studies history: **Barbara Tuchman was a well-known** *historian* **who wrote a famous book about World War I.** [35]

his·tor·i·cal [his·tôrˊə·kəl] *adj.* having to do with or existing in history: **The signing of the Declaration of Independence was an important** *historical* **event.** [24]

his·to·ry [hisˊtə·rē] *n.* events of the past, or the study or record of such events: **Queen Elizabeth I is an important figure in the** *history* **of Great Britain.** [24]

hur·ri·cane [hûrˊə·kānˊ] *n.* a severe tropical storm with strong winds and heavy rain: **A** *hurricane* **is a storm with winds of 75 or more miles per hour.** [15]

hy·drant [hīˊdrənt] *n.* a large upright pipe, connected to an underground water main, to which hoses can be attached: **It's illegal to park your car next to a fire** *hydrant.* [32]

I

i·den·ti·fi·ca·tion [ī·denˊtə·fə·kāˊshən] *n.* the act of establishing a person's identity, or the means of confirming one's identity: **A driver's license is a form of** *identification.* [33]

i·den·ti·ty [ī·denˊtə·tē] *n.* the fact of being a particular person and being recognized as that person: **Police who work undercover have to conceal their true** *identity. syn.* individuality [29]

il·lus·trate [ilˊə·strātˊ *or* i·lusˊtrātˊ] *v.* **1.** to explain by using a picture or example: **The attorney** *illustrated* **his point, using a previous case. 2.** to provide artwork to decorate or explain printed material: **Dr. Seuss's books are** *illustrated* **with funny cartoonlike characters.** [18]

in·au·gu·rate [in·ôˊgyə·rātˊ] *v.* to begin officially: **The new President will be** *inaugurated* **tomorrow.** [18]

in·ci·dent [inˊsə·dənt] *n.* a single event or occurrence, often one that is relatively unimportant: **I wrote a story about a funny** *incident* **that happened during vacation.** [21]

in·ci·den·tal·ly [inˊsə·dənˊtə·lē] *adv.* along with something else; by the way: **The committee was discussing the football team and** *incidentally* **brought up the need for new lights on the field.** [29]

in·flu·ence [inˊflōō·əns] *v.* to have an effect on; produce a change: **Don't** *influence* **their decision by giving your opinion.** [21]

in·ju·ry [inˊjər·ē] *n.* hurt, harm, or damage to a person: **An** *injury* **to her knee kept the skater from competing in the Olympics.** [14]

in·spi·ra·tion [inˊspə·rāˊshən] *n.* a feeling, idea, or desire to do something, usually aroused suddenly in a person: **The writer stared at his typewriter, waiting for** *inspiration.* [34]

in·spire [in·spīrˊ] *v.* to fill with a desire to do something: **The loss of his sweetheart** *inspired* **Edgar Allan Poe to write "Annabel Lee."** [34]

in·struc·tion [in·strukˊshən] *n.* a step or rule to be followed in doing something: **Read the** *instructions* **carefully before you begin to use the machine.** *syns.* order, direction [20]

in·tel·li·gent [in·telˊə·jənt] *adj.* having the capability to think, reason, and learn: **Rita is very** *intelligent* **and has been put in a special math program.** *syns.* bright, smart [21]

•••••••••••••••••••••••••••••••

Pronunciation Key

a	add	ō	open	th	thin
ā	ace	ô	off	th	this
â(r)	care	oi	oil	zh	vision
ä	palm	ŏŏ	took		
e	end	ōō	pool	ə	a in about
ē	equal	ou	out		e in listen
i	it	u	up		i in pencil
ī	ice	û(r)	burn		o in melon
o	odd	yōō	use		u in circus

•••••••••••••••••••••••••••••••

in·ven·tion [in·ven´chən] *n.* **1.** something brought into being for the first time: **The** *invention* **of the automobile took place in the late 1800s. 2.** something made up or untrue: **The jury thought the witness's story was an** *invention* **from start to finish.** [34]

in·ven·tor [in·ven´tər] *n.* a person who thinks up and brings into being a thing that did not exist before: **Thomas Edison was a great** *inventor.* [34]

i·vo·ry [ī´vər·ē] *n.* a hard, creamy-white substance that makes up the tusks of elephants, walruses, and certain other animals: **The** *ivory* **tusks of an elephant are a wonder of nature.** [29]

J

jag·uar [jag´wär] *n.* a large, wild cat found in Central and South America: **The** *jaguar* **is spotted like a leopard.** [4]

Ja·pan [jə·pan´] *n.* a country east of the mainland of Asia that is made up of four large islands and several smaller ones: **Tokyo is the capital of** *Japan.* [9]

Jap·a·nese [jap´ə·nēz´] **1.** *adj.* having to do with the people or culture of Japan: *Japanese* **rugs are very ornate and beautiful. 2.** *n.* the language spoken in Japan: **Midori speaks** *Japanese.* [9]

jazz [jaz] *n.* American music characterized by varied rhythm and often deliberate distortions of pitch: **Harry's favorite music is** *jazz* **because it has a great beat.** [5]

jew·el·ry [jōō´əl·rē] *n.* ornaments worn on a person's clothing or body, often made of precious metals and gems: **Mother keeps her** *jewelry* **in a satin box.** [12]

judge [juj] *n.* a person who listens to and decides cases in a court of law: **The Supreme Court of the United States has nine** *judges,* **or justices.** [17]

judg·ment [juj´mənt] *n.* the decision of a court: **The lawyer based the defense on a** *judgment* **made in an earlier case of the same kind.** [17]

ju·di·cial [jōō·dish´əl] *adj.* having to do with courts or judges: **The Supreme Court is the highest level of the United States** *judicial* **system.** [17]

K

kill·er whale [kil´ər wāl´] *n.* a large black-and-white dolphin that feeds on large fish and such water animals as seals and walruses: **The** *killer whale* **is a mammal, not a fish.** [1]

kil·o·me·ter [kil´ə·mē´tər *or* ki·lom´ə·tər] *n.* a unit of length in the metric system: **The distance of the race she planned to run was five** *kilometers.* [27]

L

la·bor [lā´bər] *v.* to work hard: **She** *labored* **all day to finish the dress in time for the school dance.** [3]

lab·o·ra·to·ry [lab´rə·tôr´ē] *n.* a room or building with special equipment for performing scientific research: **We do experiments on plants in the science** *laboratory.* [30]

league [lēg] *n.* a group of people or organizations that join together for a common purpose: **The Rams, Jets, and Titans are all members of the the National Football** *League.* [23]

length [length] *n.* the distance of a thing from one end to the other: **A football field is 100 yards in** *length.* [12]

let [let] *v.,* **letting** to allow or permit to happen: **Since we finished all our chores early, Dad is** *letting* **us go to the movies this afternoon.** [3]

li·brar·i·an [lī·brâr´ē·ən] *n.* a person who works in a library: **The school** *librarian* **helped me find information for my research paper.** [35]

li·brar·y [lī´brer´ē *or* lī´brə·rē] *n.* a room or building where a large collection of books is kept: **I went to the** *library* **to get some books for my report.** [12]

life jack·et [līf´jak´it] *n.* a life preserver that is in the form of a vest: **We always wear** *life jackets* **when we go out in the sailboat.** [1]

light·ning [līt´ning] *n.* a sudden flash of light in the sky: *Lightning* **is actually a form of electricity.** [29]

lim·ou·sine [lim´ə·zen´] *n.* a large automobile that usually has a panel of glass between the front and back seats: **The driver sits in the front seat of a** *limousine* **while the passengers sit in the back.** [30]

lis·ten [lis´(ə)n] *v.* to try to hear: **He** *listened* **silently for the sound of footsteps.** [3]

lit·er·a·ture [lit´ər·ə·chər] *n.* **1.** writing of imaginative and artistic style and quality: **This year we are studying works of American** *literature* **by such writers as Mark Twain and Emily Dickinson. 2.** printed material that advertises or promotes something: **Don asked the company to send him some** *literature* **on the new computer programs.** [12]

log·ic [loj´ik] *n.* correct reasoning of any kind: *Logic* **indicates that there were two burglars because the TV couldn't be moved by one person alone.** [32]

lone·some [lōn´səm] *adj.* not happy about being alone: **Rachel felt** *lonesome* **the first night at camp.** *syn.* lonely [11]

lunch·eon [lun´chən] *n.* lunch, especially a formal or special lunch: **Mom is planning a** *luncheon* **to celebrate my sister's birthday.** [30]

lux·u·ry [luk´shər·ē *or* lug´zhər·ē] *n.* something that gives pleasure but is not necessary: **It was a** *luxury* **for Mom, on her day off, to lie in bed late and read.** [14]

M

ma·chin·er·y [mə·shēn´(ə)rē] *n.* a collection of machines: **The John Deere Company is one of the largest makers of farm** *machinery.* [14]

mag·ni·fi·cent [mag·nif´ə·sənt] *adj.* very great, beautiful, or outstanding: **There was a** *magnificent* **view of the river valley from the top of the mountain.** [21]

ma·rine [mə·rēn´] *adj.* having to do with the ocean, ships, or boats: **A seal is a** *marine* **mammal. He got parts for his boat at a** *marine* **supply store.** [11]

mas·cu·line [mas´kyə·lin] *adj.* of or belonging to men or boys: **"Emperor," "duke," "king," and "earl" are all** *masculine* **titles.** [11]

mas·sa·cre [mas´ə·kər] *n.* a cruel and violent killing of many people: **The government of the small country feared there would be a** *massacre.* [15]

math·e·mat·ics [math´ə·mat´iks] *n.* the study of numbers, quantities, and shapes: **Arithmetic, algebra, and geometry are branches of** *mathematics.* [30]

mem·o·ran·dum [mem´ə·ran´dəm] *n.* a short letter or note written from one member of a company to another or others: **The office**

manager sent a *memorandum* to all employees informing them that the office would close early on Friday. [30]

mem·o·rize [mem´ə·rīz´] *v.* to learn by heart: **Josh** *memorized* **a small part for the school play.** [18]

me·ter [mē´tər] *n.* a unit for measuring length: **There are 1,000** *meters* **in a kilometer.** [27]

mi·cro·scope [mī´krə·skōp´] *n.* a device used to look at something too small to be seen by the eye alone: **With a** *microscope,* **researchers first saw the tiny germs that cause disease.** [32]

mis·for·tune [mis·fôr´chən] *n.* bad luck; something bad that happens: **The skier had the** *misfortune* **of breaking her ankle during the race.** [17]

miss [mis] *v.* **1.** to not do what is expected or intended: **I** *missed* **one question on the test but still got a good grade. 2.** to feel lonesome because some one is not there: **The class** *missed* **our teacher, Mr. Johnson, when he was home with the flu.** [2]

mis·sion·ar·y [mish´ən·er´ē] *n.* a person who goes out to teach and spread a particular religion, usually in a foreign country: **Father Junípero Serra was a** *missionary* **who went from Spain to live among the people of Mexico and California.** [14]

mist [mist] *n.* a cloud of very tiny drops of moisture in the air: **After the sudden shower, a light** *mist* **filled the air.** [2]

moc·ca·sin [mok´ə·sin] *n.* a slipperlike shoe with a soft sole and no heel: *Moccasins* **may be adorned with embroidery or beading.** [15]

mon·o·logue [mon´ə·lôg´] *n.* a speech, part in a play, or series of jokes told by one person: **The comedian started his performance with a** *monologue* **about air travel.** [32]

Pronunciation Key

a	add	ō	open	th	thin
ā	ace	ô	off	th	this
â(r)	care	oi	oil	zh	vision
ä	palm	ŏŏ	took		
e	end	ōō	pool	ə	a in about
ē	equal	ou	out		e in listen
i	it	u	up		i in pencil
ī	ice	û(r)	burn		o in melon
o	odd	yōō	use		u in circus

mo·nop·o·ly [mə·nop′ə·lē] *n.* a company or group of companies that controls the supply of a product or service: **For many years, AT&T had a** *monopoly* **on telephone service in the United States.** [28]

mo·not·o·nous [mə·not′ə·nəs] *adj.* continuing without change at the same level: **The speaker had a** *monotonous* **voice, and it was hard to focus on what he was saying.** *syns.* boring, tiring [28]

moon·light [mōōn′līt′] *n.* the light that comes from the moon: **The** *moonlight* **cast a silver glow over the landscape.** [1]

mos·qui·to [məs·kē′tō] *n.* a small, flying insect that is found especially in hot, damp places: **The** *mosquito* **can be a carrier of diseases such as malaria and yellow fever.** [4]

mus·cle [mus′əl] *n.* strong, elastic body tissue that makes body parts move: **Andrea joined a weight-lifting class to build** *muscle*. [16]

mus·cu·lar [mus′kyə·lər] *adj.* having to do with the muscles: **A loss or impairment of voluntary** *muscular* **power is called paralysis.** [16]

mu·si·cian [myōō·zish′ən] *n.* a person who plays or sings music: **The** *musician* **came on stage and began to tune her instrument.** [35]

my·thol·o·gy [mi·thol′ə·jē] *n.* a group of myths and legends: **In Greek** *mythology*, **Zeus is the ruler of all the gods.** [32]

N

nec·es·sar·y [nes′ə·ser′ē] *adj.* that which must be done or had: **Food and shelter are** *necessary* **for life.** *syns.* needed, required [20]

neck·tie [nek′tī′] *n.* a long, narrow strip of cloth that is tied under the collar of a shirt: **Bobby's brother always wore a colorful** *necktie*. [30]

nurs·er·y [nûr′sər·ē] *n.* 1. a room or place for babies: **We looked through the window of the hospital** *nursery* **at all the brand-new babies.** 2. a place where plants are grown and sold: **Dad bought two rose bushes from the** *nursery*. [14]

O

Oc·to·ber [ok·tō′bər] *n.* the tenth month of the year: **Jill's birthday is on the eighth of** *October*. [28]

oc·to·pus [ok′tə·pəs] *n.* a sea animal with a soft body and eight arms: **The** *octopus* **is a type of shellfish, although it does not have a shell.** [28]

of·fer [ô′fər] *v.* to present something or a service: **She** *offered* **her guest a cup of tea.** [22]

off·shore [ôf′shôr′] 1. *adj.* away from the shore: **The** *offshore* **breeze pushed our sailboat swiftly.** 2. *adv.* a distance from the shore: **The ship is anchored** *offshore*. [1]

o·mit [ō·mit′] *v.* to leave out; not include or do: **Be sure to check the guest list to make sure we did not** *omit* **anyone.** [22]

o·pos·sum [ə·pos′əm *or* pos′əm] *n.* a small, furry mammal that is native to North America: **When they are in danger,** *opossums* **lie motionless and appear to be dead.** [15]

op·po·site [op′ə·zit] 1. *n.* something that is totally different from another thing: **Up is the** *opposite* **of down.** 2. *adj.* across from: **Iowa and Illinois are on** *opposite* **sides of the Mississippi River.** [20]

or·gan·i·za·tion [ôr′gən·ə·zā′shən] *n.* 1. a group of people joined together for a purpose: **A corporation is a large business** *organization*. 2. the putting together of things according to a system: **The new secretary did not understand the** *organization* **of the files.** [33]

or·gan·ize [ôr′gən·īz′] *v.* to put things together in a certain order: **When Ruth** *organized* **her closet, she put all her shoes in a neat row on one side.** [18]

o·ver·night [ō′vər·nīt′] *adj.* during or through the night: **We are going on an** *overnight* **trip and plan to return tomorrow night.** [1]

P

pain [pān] *n.* a feeling of hurt or great discomfort: **The dentist numbed Manuel's mouth so he wouldn't feel** *pain* **when she filled his tooth.** [2]

pane [pān] *n.* a sheet of glass set into a window or door frame: **We all watched the rain beat on the window** *panes*. [2]

par·a·chute [par′ə·shōōt′] *n.* a large piece of umbrella-shaped cloth that unfolds in midair to slow the fall of someone from a great height: **A** *parachute* **descends about 15 feet per second or slightly faster, depending on the weight it carries.** [30]

par·a·graph [par´ə·graf´] *n.* a section of a piece of writing that starts on a new line that is usually indented from the other lines: **The topic of a *paragraph* is often stated in the first sentence.** [27]

par·a·lyze [par´ə·līz´] *v.* **1.** to make unable to move or function: **A serious spinal injury can *paralyze* a person. 2.** to make helpless: **A power failure would *paralyze* the entire city.** [18]

par·ti·cle [pär´ti·kəl] *n.* a tiny piece or bit: **There were dust *particles* on the windowsill.** [16]

par·tic·u·lar [pər·tik´yə·lər] *adj.* **1.** apart from others: **Each team must select a *particular* topic for the debate. 2.** being a certain one: **Hank searched all over, trying to find the *particular* wood he needed for his airplane model.** *syns.* specific, unusual [16]

pa·ti·o [pat´ē·ō *or* pä´te·ō] *n.* an outdoor space next to a house that is usually tiled or paved: **We use our *patio* for outdoor dining and relaxing.** [4]

pend·ing [pen´ding] *prep.* while awaiting: **The man charged with the crime was held in jail *pending* his trial.** [34]

pen·e·trate [pen´ə·trāt´] *v.* to go into or pass through: **The doctor warned that the needle would *penetrate* the skin.** [29]

per·form [pər·fôrm´] *v.* **1.** to carry out a certain work or action: **The team *performed* the play exactly as they had in practice. 2.** to act, sing, play a musical instrument, or do another artistic endeavor before the public: **That actor *performs* in many movies and TV shows.** [34]

per·form·ance [pər·fôr´məns] *n.* a play, program, or other entertainment that is presented before an audience: **There is a *performance* of *Swan Lake* at the ballet tonight.** [5]

per·i·scope [per´ə·skōp´] *n.* a device that enables a viewer to see things that are around a corner or otherwise blocked from view: **A *periscope* is used in a submarine to see things above the water.** [32]

per·mit [*v.* pər·mit´; *n.* pûr´mit] *v.,* **permitting 1.** *v.* to agree that a person may do something: **Cell phones are not *permitted* in this theater. 2.** *v.* to make possible; allow to happen: **I'll bake cookies tomorrow, if time *permits*. 3.** *n.* a written statement from some authority allowing something: **You need a *permit* to fish in the lake.** [3, 22]

pho·to·graph [fō´tə·graf´] *n.* a picture made with a camera: **Something must be wrong with the camera; every *photograph* from our trip came out fuzzy.** [27]

pho·tog·ra·phy [fə·tog´rə·fē] *n.* the art of taking pictures with a camera: **Still *photography* produces pictures in which there is no motion.** [27]

phy·si·cian [fi·zish´ən] *n.* a person who is licensed to practice medicine: **Dr. Smith is our family *physician*.** *syn.* doctor [35]

pi·an·ist [pē·an´ist *or* pē´ə·nist] *n.* a person who plays the piano: **Arthur Rubinstein was a great classical *pianist*.** [5]

pin·na·cle [pin´ə·kəl] *n.* the highest point of achievement: **Michael Jordan retired from pro basketball at the *pinnacle* of his career.** [15]

pi·o·neer [pī´ə·nir´] *n.* one of the first people to live in a new land: **In the 1800s many *pioneers* crossed this country in covered wagons to settle in the West.** [35]

plaque [plak] *n.* **1.** a flat piece of wood or metal with an inscription on it: **After ten years of service, an employee at our company receives a bonus and a *plaque*. 2.** a thin film on the surface of teeth caused by food: **The dental assistant uses a special tool to scrape *plaque* from the teeth.** [23]

plat·i·num [plat´ə·nəm] *n.* a valuable metal that resembles silver: ***Platinum* is often used in jewelry.** [29]

pol·i·ti·cian [pol´ə·tish´ən] *n.* a person who is elected to public office or who is otherwise involved in politics: **A mayor is a *politician*.** [35]

pop·u·lar [pop´yə·lər] *adj.* well-liked; enjoyed by many people: *The Lion King* was a very *popular* movie. [16]

•••••••••••••••••••••••••••••••

Pronunciation Key

a	add	ō	open	th	thin
ā	ace	ô	off	th	this
â(r)	care	oi	oil	zh	vision
ä	palm	oŏ	took		
e	end	oō	pool	ə	a in about
ē	equal	ou	out		e in listen
i	it	u	up		i in pencil
ī	ice	û(r)	burn		o in melon
o	odd	yōō	use		u in circus

•••••••••••••••••••••••••••••••

pop·u·la·tion [pop´yə·lā´shən] *n.* the total number of people who live in a place, or these people as a group: **Almost the entire *population* of the town turned out for the parade.** [16]

por·trait [pôr´trit *or* por´trāt´] *n.* a rather formal painting or photograph of a person: **A *portrait* usually shows the face and upper part of the body.** [23]

po·si·tion [pə·zish´ən] *n.* the place at which a person or thing is: **Tanya took her *position* at the head of the line.** [20]

pos·si·bil·i·ty [pos´ə·bil´ə·tē] *n.* the fact of being possible: **Do you think it is a *possibility* that humans could live on the moon?** [33]

prai·rie [prâr´ē] *n.* a large, open area of flat or hilly land that is covered with tall grasses: **The *prairie* of the midwestern United States has been called a "sea of grass."** [23]

prej·u·dice [prej´ŏŏ·dis] *n.* the judging of something by a general opinion formed beforehand rather than by the facts or evidence of that particular situation: **It is a form of *prejudice* to dislike someone you do not know because of his or her ethnicity.** [17]

prob·a·bly [prob´ə·blē] *adv.* almost certain or definite: **From the look of those dark clouds, I'd say that it will *probably* rain today.** [12]

psy·chi·a·trist [sī·kī´ə·trist] *n.* a doctor who is specially trained to treat diseases and conditions of the mind: **A *psychiatrist* helps people solve their problems.** [35]

psy·chol·o·gy [sī·kol´ə·jē] *n.* the scientific study of mental processes and behavior: ***Psychology* has increased our knowledge of why people behave as they do.** [32]

Q

quart [kwôrt] *n.* a unit of liquid measure: **There are two pints in a *quart*.** [28]

quar·ters [kwôr´tərz] *n.* a place to live or stay: **The Red Cross set up temporary *quarters* for the flood victims in the town hall.** [28]

quar·tet [kwôr·tet´] *n.* a group of four singers or musicians who perform together: **Walt sings tenor with a barbershop *quartet*.** [28]

R

real [rēl] *adj.* **1.** not imagined or made up: **Everyone calls her Buff, even though her *real* name is Sandra.** *syn.* true **2.** not artificial: **It's** hard to tell the difference between the artificial pearls and the *real* ones. *syn.* genuine [2]

re·al·ize [rē´əl·īz´] *v.* to be aware of or know about: **The runner didn't *realize* how close she was to the finish line until she heard the crowd cheering for her.** [18]

re·ceipt [ri·sēt´] *n.* a written statement that something has been received: **Be sure you keep the *receipt* in case the blouse doesn't fit.** [25]

re·cep·tion [ri·sep´shən] *n.* **1.** the fact of receiving: **The band got a warm *reception* from the audience. 2.** the quality of signals received by a television or radio: **You get better *reception* on your television if you have cable.** [25]

re·cess [ri·ses´ *or* rē´ses] *n.* **1.** a time when work stops: **When the weather is nice, we go outside and play marbles during *recess*. The judge declared a short *recess* for lunch. 2.** a secret or hidden place: **She found a *recess* in the wall where she could hide the letter.** [20]

rec·og·nize [rek´əg·nīz´] *v.* to become aware of a person or a thing as someone or something already known: **Celia hoped she would *recognize* the bracelet Jerome found as the one that had been taken from her locker.** *syn.* identify [18]

rec·om·men·da·tion [rek´ə·men·dā´shən] *n.* the act of speaking in favor of someone or something: **Her boss gave her a letter of *recommendation* saying what a good worker she was.** [33]

rec·tan·gle [rek´tang´gəl] *n.* a figure having four straight sides and four right angles: **The opposite sides of a *rectangle* are parallel and are equal in length.** [16]

rec·tan·gu·lar [rek·tang´gyə·lər] *adj.* having the shape of a rectangle: **A football field is a *rectangular* area.** [16]

red·dish [red´ish] *adj.* tinged with red: **The setting sun gave a *reddish* hue to the sky.** [11]

reel [rēl] **1.** *v.* to be thrown off balance; spin around: **The other boxer will *reel* from the force of Mike's blow.** *syns.* sway, whirl **2.** *n.* a spool on which something is wound: **After the fish got away, Cindy rewound the line on her *reel*. 3.** *n.* a spirited folk dance: **We learned to do the Virginia *reel* in our dance class.** [2]

re·fer [ri·fûr´] *v.* to direct attention to: **Mom sent the new neighbor to our doctor, but the doctor *referred* him to a specialist.** [22]

ref·er·ence [ref´ər·əns *or* ref´rəns] *n.* **1.** something that directs a reader to another source of information: **The article in the magazine made a *reference* to a previous article. 2.** a work containing facts or useful information: **A dictionary, an encyclopedia, and a thesaurus are all *references*.** [12, 22]

re·form [ri·fôrm´] *v.* to change for the better: **The new mayor *reformed* the city government.** [34]

re·frig·er·a·tor [ri·frij´ə·rā´tər] *n.* an appliance used to keep things cold: **Our new *refrigerator* has an ice-making machine in the door.** [30]

reg·u·lar [reg´yə·lər] *adj.* happening over and over in the same way: **After vacation, we slipped back into our *regular* routine.** *syn.* normal [16]

reg·u·la·tion [reg´yə·lā´shən] *n.* something that directs or controls, such as a law or rule: **A fire *regulation* poster was hung by each elevator.** [16]

re·ha·bil·i·ta·tion [re´hə·bil´ə·tāsh´ən] *n.* the act of restoring to a former, often better, condition: **The *rehabilitation* of an old building is often a very long and expensive responsibility. After she broke her leg, she had to go through a long period of physical *rehabilitation*.** [33]

re·hears·al [ri·hûr´səl] *n.* a practice session before a performance: **The photographer took pictures of the final dress *rehearsal* of the opera.** [5]

re·luc·tant [ri·luk´tənt] *adj.* not wanting to do something: **The witness seemed nervous and *reluctant* to answer questions.** [21]

re·sign [ri·zīn´] *v.* to give up a job or an office: **Jan will *resign* from her job at the bank.** [25]

res·ig·na·tion [rez´ig·nā´shən] *n.* the giving up of one's job or office: **She will announce her *resignation* at the end of the week.** [25]

res·pi·ra·tion [res´pə·rā´shən] *n.* the process of breathing: **In mammals, *respiration* occurs in the lungs.** [34]

re·spon·si·bil·i·ty [ri·spon´sə·bil´ə·tē] *n.,* **responsibilities** the fact of being responsible for something: **Two of the secretary's *responsibilities* are to file reports and to answer the phone.** [33]

res·tau·rant [res´tər·ənt *or* res´tə·ränt´] *n.* a place in which meals are made and sold to customers: **It's expensive for our whole family to eat out, so we go to a *restaurant* only on special occasions.** [29]

re·vise [ri·vīz´] *v.* to correct errors and bring up to date: **Since it was first published, this dictionary has been *revised* many times to reflect our changing language.** [20]

rev·o·lu·tion·ar·y [rev´ə·loo´shən·er´ē] *adj.* having to do with or causing a revolution: **The Boston Tea Party was a *revolutionary* action taken by the American colonists.** [14]

ro·de·o [rō´dē·ō *or* rō·dā´ō] *n.* a show that has contests in the skills a cowhand must have, such as horseback riding: **A big crowd went to see the *rodeo* when it came to our town.** [4]

ru·in [roo´in] *v.* to cause destruction: **Hannah waded through the mud and *ruined* her dress shoes.** [3]

S

sail·boat [sāl´bōt´] *n.* a boat that is moved by the action of the wind on its sails: **The body of a *sailboat* is called the hull.** [1]

scen·er·y [sē´nər·ē] *n.* **1.** the general way a place looks, especially an outdoor place: **The *scenery* at Yosemite National Park is breathtaking. 2.** the stage setting for a play: **The *scenery* gave the audience a sense of the small room.** [14]

sci·en·tist [sī´ən·tist] *n.* a person who works in the field of science: **A *scientist* uses observation and experimentation to develop new theories.** [35]

scope [skōp] *n.* the range of an idea or action: **The mayor said intervening in the strike was beyond the *scope* of his authority.** [32]

Pronunciation Key

a	add	ō	open	th	thin
ā	ace	ô	off	t̶h̶	this
â(r)	care	oi	oil	zh	vision
ä	palm	o͝o	took		
e	end	o͞o	pool	ə	a in about
ē	equal	ou	out		e in listen
i	it	u	up		i in pencil
ī	ice	û(r)	burn		o in melon
o	odd	yo͞o	use		u in circus

sea·weed [sē´wēd´] *n.* the many kinds of plants that grow in the ocean: **After the storm, they cleared off the** *seaweed* **that had washed up on the shore.** [1]

self·ish [sel´fish] *adj.* caring more about one's own needs than those of others: **I think it's** *selfish* **of Nancy not to let anyone borrow her books.** [11]

sep·a·rate [*v.* sep´ə·rāt´; *adj.* sep´ər·it *or* sep´rit] **1.** *v.* to keep apart: **She will** *separate* **the children. 2.** *adj.* apart from one another: **The garage is** *separate* **from the house.** [12]

shone [shōn] *v.* gave off a bright light: **The stars** *shone* **brightly overhead.** *syn.* glowed [2]

shoot [shoot] *v.* **1.** to fire a weapon: **The police officer would go to the range and** *shoot* **at targets. 2.** to score a point in certain games: **Can you** *shoot* **the ball into the basket? 3.** to play, as certain games: **Shall we** *shoot* **a game of pool?** [2]

show [shō] *v.* to allow to be seen: **I'll** *show* **you my new magic trick.** [2]

sign [sīn] **1.** *n.* an object or symbol that stands for something else: **The** *sign* **for division is ÷. 2.** *n.* an indication, as of a condition: **Flowers blooming is a** *sign* **of spring. 3.** *v.* to write one's name on: **I always** *sign* **my artwork with my initials.** [25]

sig·na·ture [sig´nə·chər] *n.* a person's name in that person's own handwriting: **The sales-clerk checked the** *signature* **on the credit card.** [25]

si·mul·ta·ne·ous·ly [sī´məl·tā´nē·əs·lē] *adv.* at the same time: **The fireworks exploded, and people in the crowd cheered** *simul-taneously.* [33]

sof·ten [sôf´ən] *v.* to make softer: **Mary kept the ice cream out until it** *softened* **enough to be served.** *[25]*

soft·ly [sôft´lē] *adv.* quietly; not roughly: **People need to speak** *softly* **in the library.** [25]

Spain [spān] *n.* a country in southwest Europe: **The Olympics were held in** *Spain* **in 1992.** [9]

Span·ish [span´ish] **1.** *adj.* having to do with Spain: **We ate** *Spanish* **food for dinner last night. 2.** *n.* the language spoken in Spain and in countries that were once ruled by Spain: **The part of the movie spoken in** *Spanish* **had subtitles on the screen.** [9]

spe·cial·ist [spesh´əl·ist] *n.* a person who concen-trates on one limited area of a larger activity: **Dr. James is a** *specialist* **in eye surgery.** [17]

spe·cif·ic [spi·sif´ik] *adj.* naming a certain one or ones; clearly stated: **"Plants" is a general subject for a report; "tomatoes" is a more** *specific* **topic.** [17]

spec·i·fi·ca·tion [spes´ə·fə·kā´shən] *n.* a detailed and exact presentation of something: **The carpenter drew up** *specifications* **for the new cabinets.** [17]

stam·pede [stam·pēd´] *n.* a sudden, wild rush of animals or people: **The** *stampede* **of the frightened cattle sounded like thunder.** [4]

stra·te·gic [strə·tē´jik] *adj.* having to do with or important to a particular plan: **The chess player made a** *strategic* **move when he gave up a knight.** [241]

strat·e·gy [strat´ə·jē] *n.* a careful, overall plan: **The team changed its** *strategy* **and won the game.** [24]

straw·ber·ry [strô´ber´ē] *n.* a small, heart-shaped, red berry with a sweet taste: **The** *strawberry* **is a small plant of the rose family.** [1]

strength [streng(k)th] *n.* the quality of being strong: **Mel didn't have the** *strength* **to lift the box.** [12]

struc·ture [struk´chər] *n.* something that is built: **All** *structures* **near the airport must be less than three stories high.** [20]

stud·y [stud´ē] *v.* to try to understand or learn something: **Samantha is** *studying* **to be an engineer.** [3]

sub·ma·rine [sub´mə·rēn´] *n.* a ship that can travel underwater: **This** *submarine* **is designed for defensive use.** [30]

sub·mit [səb·mit´] *v.* to give in to a power or authority: **The rebels would not** *submit* **to government forces.** *syn.* yield [22]

sub·stance [sub´stəns] *n.* any material that something is made of: **A diamond is a hard** *substance.* [21]

sub·trac·tion [səb·trak´shən] *n.* the taking away of one number from another: **Subtraction is finding the difference between two numbers.** [22]

suc·ceed [sək·sēd´] *v.* **1.** to do very well at something: **The team** *succeeded* **in winning the championship after a number of losing seasons. 2.** to come next; follow after: **Harry S Truman** *succeeded* **Franklin D. Roosevelt as President of the United States.** [20]

suede [swād] *n.* a soft leather with a fuzzy nap on one side: **Jackets made of** *suede* **are very soft.** [2]

suf·fer [suf´ər] v. to endure pain or misery: **I will** suffer **from a broken heart if I'm not careful.** [22]

sus·pend [sə·spend´] v. to hang down from above: **The chandelier was** suspended **from the ceiling.** [34]

swal·low [swol´ō] v. to take food through the mouth into the stomach: **The dog** swallowed **its dinner.** [3]

sway [swā] v. to swing slowly back and forth: **The tall grass** swayed **softly in the breeze.** [2]

syl·la·ble [sil´ə·bəl] n. a single sound that forms a word or part of a word: **The accent is on the first** syllable **of the word "swallow."** [15]

T

tech·ni·cian [tek·nish´ən] n. a person who has special training in a technical field: **Abby was a laboratory** technician **for ten years before she decided to be a full-time mother.** [35]

tech·nique [tek·nēk´] n. a particular way of doing something or dealing with a problem: **The difficulty of her program showed the pianist's mastery of** technique. [23]

tech·nol·o·gy [tek·nol´ə·jē] n. the use of scientific principles and tools to solve practical problems: **The space program is a good example of the success of** technology **and engineering.** [32]

teen·ag·er [tēn´ā´jər] n. a person between the ages of thirteen and nineteen: **Today,** teenagers **make up the largest audience for many TV shows.** [30]

tel·e·scope [tel´ə·skōp´] n. an instrument that magnifies objects seen at a great distance: **In the 1600s, the Italian astronomer Galileo built a** telescope **through which he saw the rings of Saturn.** [32]

tel·e·vise [tel´ə·vīz´] v. to send out a signal or program by television: **Tonight's baseball game will be** televised **on Channel 10.** [20]

tem·per·a·ture [tem´pər·ə·chər or tem´prə·chər] n. the level of heat or cold in a place or object: **The normal body** temperature **of a human is about 98.6 degrees Fahrenheit.** [12]

ten·ta·tive·ly [ten´tə·tiv·lē] adv. with hesitation as though unsure: **She put her foot** tentatively **on the ice, not sure if it would bear her weight.** [29]

ter·ri·to·ry [ter´ə·tôr´ē] n. an area of land: **In the early 1700s most of the** territory **along** the Mississippi River was claimed by France. [14]

ther·mom·e·ter [thər·mom´ə·tər] n. an instrument used to measure temperature: **Mom used a meat** thermometer **to see if the turkey was fully cooked.** [27]

tide [tīd] n. the regular rise and fall of the level of the ocean: **The** tide **changes from high to low and back again about every twelve hours.** [2]

tie [tī] v. to fasten, as with string or rope: **We** tied **the bundle of firewood together with heavy wire.** [2]

to·bac·co [tə·bak´ō] n. a tall plant with large leaves that are dried and used for smoking and chewing: Tobacco **was grown in the southern colonies and exported to England.** [15]

to·ma·to [tə·mā´tō or tə·mä´tō] n. a plump, juicy red or yellow fruit with seeds and a smooth skin, widely used as a vegetable: **I like to eat lettuce and** tomato **on a hamburger.** [4]

to·mor·row [tə·mor´ō] n. the next day after today: **If today is Monday,** tomorrow **will be Tuesday.** [15]

tor·na·do [tôr·nā´dō] n. a violent wind storm that creates a dark, twisting, funnel-shaped cloud: **A** tornado **follows a narrow path along the ground, lifting objects in its path with great force.** [4]

tor·til·la [tôr·tē´yä] n. a flat, round Mexican bread made from corn or wheat flour: Tortillas **can be filled with meat and folded to make several tasty Mexican dishes.** [4]

trans·fer [trans´fər or trans·für´] v. to move or send from one place to another: **To get downtown, you** transfer **here from the No. 11 bus to the No. 6.** [22]

Pronunciation Key

a	add	ō	open	th	thin
ā	ace	ô	off	th	this
â(r)	care	oi	oil	zh	vision
ä	palm	o͝o	took		
e	end	o͞o	pool	ə	a in about
ē	equal	ou	out		e in listen
i	it	u	up		i in pencil
ī	ice	û(r)	burn		o in melon
o	odd	yo͞o	use		u in circus

trans·form [trans·fôrm´] *v.* to change in shape or appearance: **At the end of the story, an ugly frog was** *transformed* **into a handsome prince.** [34]

tran·sis·tor [tran·zis´tər] *n.* a small electronic device that controls the flow of electricity in a computer, radio, television, or the like: *Transistors* **have taken the place of the less-reliable vacuum tubes.** [34]

trans·mis·sion [trans·mish´ən] *n.* **1.** the sending of something from one place to another: **She ordered a** *transmission* **of funds to the bank in Sweden.** *syn.* transfer **2.** the sending out of radio or television signals: **The storm must be interferring with the satellite** *transmission.* **3.** the mechanism in a car that sends power from the engine to the wheels: **The auto mechanic said he did extensive work to my car's** *transmission.* [22]

treas·ur·y [trezh´ər·ē] *n.* the place where an organization's funds are kept and managed: **There is enough money in the student council** *treasury* **for a party.** [14]

tri·an·gle [trī´ang´gəl] *n.* **1.** a flat figure with three sides and three angles: **The "yield" sign at an intersection has the characteristic shape of a** *triangle.* **2.** a musical instrument made from a metal bar that is bent into this shape: *Triangles* **make a bell-like sound when struck with a small stick.** [16, 28]

tri·an·gu·lar [trī¯ang´gyə·lər] *adj.* having to do with, or shaped like, a triangle: **An arrowhead has a** *triangular* **shape.** [16]

tri·cy·cle [trī˘sik·əl] *n.* a small three-wheeled vehicle that is usually moved with pedals: **Most children learn to ride a** *tricycle* **before they ride a bike.** [28]

tri·o [trē´o] *n.* a group or set of three: **A** *trio* **of entertainers played the keyboard, bass guitar, and drums for our school dance.** [28]

tri·ple [trip´əl] **1.** *adj.* having three parts: **I ordered a** *triple* **cone, with vanilla, chocolate, and strawberry ice cream. 2.** *n.* in baseball, a hit that allows the batter to reach third base: **In the ninth inning, Jason hit a** *triple* **to win the game.** [28]

trum·pet [trum´pit] *n.* a musical instrument made from a brass tube shaped into a loop with a wide opening at one end: **One plays the** *trumpet* **by blowing into a mouthpiece and pressing on valves.** [5]

twelfth [twelfth] *adj.* next after the eleventh:

Eleven of the eggs in the carton were perfect, but the *twelfth* **one had a cracked shell.** [12]

type·writ·er [tīp´rī˘tər] *n.* a machine that prints letters on paper, using keys that are pressed with the fingers: **During the twentieth century many writers used a** *typewriter,* **but today they usually use a computer.** [1]

U

um·brel·la [um·brel´ə] *n.* a circular piece of cloth or plastic stretched on a folding frame that is held overhead for protection from rain or sun: **I keep an** *umbrella* **in my backpack in case of rain.** [15]

un·der·wa·ter [un´dər·wô´tər *or* un´dər·wo´tər] *adj.* used, done, or found below the surface of the water: **The "Chunnel" is an** *underwater* **tunnel going across the English Channel between France and Great Britain.** [1]

un·doubt·ed·ly [un·dou´tid·lē] *adv.* without a doubt: **That was** *undoubtedly* **the worst movie I have ever seen.** *syn.* certainly [17]

un·for·tu·nate [un·fôr´chə·nit] *adj.* without luck: **Bob had an** *unfortunate* **trip; he got on the wrong bus and ended up on the other side of town.** [17]

un·i·form [yōō´nə·fôrm´] **1.** *n.* a special set of clothes that identifies a person as a member of a certain group: **Admission to this museum is free to military personnel in** *uniform.* **2.** *adj.* being the same; having the same size, rate, form, and so on: **All the lines had a** *uniform* **length of four inches.** [34]

u·nique [yōō·nēk´] *adj.* like no other; being the only one of its kind: **Hawaii is** *unique* **among the states of the United States because it is a group of volcanic islands located in the central Pacific Ocean.** [23]

V

vague [vāg] *adj.* not clear or definite: **When the teacher asked where the state of Nevada is, Dave gave the** *vague* **answer, "in the West."** [23]

va·nil·la [və·nil´ə] *n.* a flavoring made from the dried seed pods of a certain tropical plant: *Vanilla* **is used in cakes, candies, ice cream, and other sweets.** [4]

veg·e·ta·ble [vej´(ə·)tə·bəl] *n.* any plant or plant part that is eaten for food, such as peas, beans, lettuce, corn, carrots, or potatoes: **My favorite** *vegetables* **are spinach and green beans.** [12]

ve·hi·cle [vē´ə·kəl] *n.* anything used to move or carry people or goods, usually having wheels or runners: **An overhead sign indicated that the garage could not accommodate** *vehicles* **over eight feet high.** [16]

ve·hic·u·lar [vē·hik´yə·lər] *adj.* having to do with a vehicle or vehicles: **This street will be closed to** *vehicular* **traffic all day today.** [16]

vic·to·ry [vik´tər·ē] *n.* the act of winning a battle, struggle, or contest: **We held a party to celebrate our** *victory* **over the top team in the league.** [14]

Vi·et·nam [vē·et·näm´] *n.* a country in southeast Asia, on the South China Sea: **Hanoi is the capital of** *Vietnam.* [9]

Vi·et·nam·ese [vē·et´nə·mēz´] **1.** *adj.* having to do with the people or culture of Vietnam: **The** *Vietnamese* **flag has a yellow star on a red background. 2.** *n.* the language spoken in Vietnam: **Chi's grandmother spoke only in** *Vietnamese.* [9]

vi·o·lin [vɪ˘·ə·lin´] *n.* a musical instrument with a wooden body, played by drawing a bow across four strings: **The** *violin* **is an important instrument in a symphony orchestra.** [5]

vi·sion [vizh´ən] *n.* **1.** the power or ability to see: **Joel wears glasses to improve his** *vision.* **2.** the power or ability to think of what things will be like in the future: **That city showed great** *vision* **in developing a rapid-transit system twenty years ago.** [20]

vis·i·tor [viz´ə·tər] *n.* a person who goes to see someone or someplace for a time: **The park is closed to** *visitors* **after nightfall.** [20]

vol·un·teer [vol´ən·tir´] **1.** *n.* a person who willingly does a job without pay: **On weekends,** Jenny is a hospital *volunteer;* **she delivers flowers and mail to the patients. 2.** *v.* to offer without being forced to do so: **The teacher asked, "Which of you will** *volunteer* **to read your essay out loud?"** [35]

voy·age [voi´ij] *n.* a trip or journey, especially a long trip over water: **My dream vacation would be an ocean** *voyage* **to Alaska.** [23]

W

wat·er·mel·on [wô´tər·mel´ən *or* wot´ər·mel´ən] *n.* a large melon that has sweet, juicy red or pink flesh, many seeds, and a hard green skin: **We always eat** *watermelon* **on the Fourth of July.** [1]

whole·some [hōl´səm] *adj.* **1.** good for the health: **Fruit and granola bars are** *wholesome* **snacks.** *syn.* healthful **2.** good for the mind or character: **That movie provides** *wholesome* **family fun.** [11]

wild·life [wıld´lıf´] *n.* animals and plants that live naturally in a wild area: **The swamp near our house has many different kinds of** *wildlife.* [1]

●●●●●●●●●●●●●●●●●●●●●●●●●●●●●●●

Pronunciation Key

a	add	ō	open	th	thin
ā	ace	ô	off	th	this
â(r)	care	oi	oil	zh	vision
ä	palm	o͝o	took		
e	end	o͞o	pool	ə	a in about
ē	equal	ou	out		e in listen
i	it	u	up	'	i in pencil
ī	ice	û(r)	burn		o in melon
o	odd	yo͞o	use		u in circus

●●●●●●●●●●●●●●●●●●●●●●●●●●●●●●●

Your Word Logs

This is a special place where you can keep track of words that are important to you.

Lesson Word Log

pages 110–115

This is the place for you to list words you need to study. List the words from any lesson that needs your special attention. Then they'll be easy to find when you're ready to study them. There's a page for each unit of your spelling book.

Personal Word Log

pages 116–118

You choose the words to list on these pages. It's up to you! Include new words, words that are especially interesting, and any other words you want to remember. Group the words into categories any way you like, and write them on these pages.

➤ words from other languages
➤ vivid words
➤ craft words
➤ food words
➤ tricky words
➤ big words
➤ music words
➤ art words
➤ science and math words
➤ social studies words
➤ words you would like to use when you write
➤ words you are curious about
➤ words you have trouble pronouncing
➤ technical words like computer words and business words

Unit 1 : Lesson Word Log

List the words you missed on the pretest. It's a good idea to include other words from the lesson that you aren't sure you can spell correctly.

LESSON 1

LESSON 2

LESSON 3

LESSON 4

LESSON 5

Unit 2: Lesson Word Log

List the words you missed on the pretest. It's a good idea to include other words from the lesson that you aren't sure you can spell correctly.

LESSON 7

LESSON 8

LESSON 9

LESSON 10

LESSON 11

LESSON 12

Unit 3: Lesson Word Log

List the words you missed on the pretest. It's a good idea to include other words from the lesson that you aren't sure you can spell correctly.

LESSON 14

LESSON 15

LESSON 16

LESSON 17

LESSON 18

Unit 4: Lesson Word Log

List the words you missed on the pretest. It's a good idea to include other words from the lesson that you aren't sure you can spell correctly.

LESSON 20

LESSON 21

LESSON 22

LESSON 23

LESSON 24

LESSON 25

Unit 5: Lesson Word Log

List the words you missed on the pretest. It's a good idea to include other words from the lesson that you aren't sure you can spell correctly.

LESSON 27

LESSON 28

LESSON 29

LESSON 30

Unit 6: Lesson Word Log

List the words you missed on the pretest. It's a good idea to include other words from the lesson that you aren't sure you can spell correctly.

LESSON 32

LESSON 33

LESSON 34

LESSON 35

Personal Word Log

You choose the words to list on these pages. It's up to you! Include new words, words that are especially interesting, and any other words you want to remember.

WORD AND NOTES

WORD AND NOTES

WORD AND NOTES

WORD AND NOTES

WORD AND NOTES

Personal Word Log

You choose the words to list on these pages. It's up to you! Include new words, words that are especially interesting, and any other words you want to remember.

WORD AND NOTES

WORD AND NOTES

WORD AND NOTES

WORD AND NOTES

WORD AND NOTES

Personal Word Log

You choose the words to list on these pages. It's up to you! Include new words, words that are especially interesting, and any other words you want to remember.

WORD AND NOTES

WORD AND NOTES

WORD AND NOTES

WORD AND NOTES

WORD AND NOTES